POODLE

An Illustrated History of the
Reign of Ikus P.Q.R.S. Aroonus

Photograph by Brian Lusk

IKUS P.Q.R.S. AROONUS

POODLE

An Illustrated History of the Reign of Ikus P.Q.R.S. Aroonus

Martha B. Lusk

CENTENNIAL PRESS • LINCOLN

Library of Congress Catalog Card No.: 77-073433

ISBN 0-8220-1662-1 (hard-cover edition)
ISBN 0-8220-1664-8 (paperback edition)

Centennial Press is a division of
Cliffs Notes, Inc., Box 80728, Lincoln, Nebraska, 68501.

CONTENTS

1. HERE IS YOUR POODLE PUPPY   1

2. THE LADY   10

3. CLOWN   21

4. COMMUNICATION   33

5. BOSS IKE   47

6. JUST ONE TIME   64

7. HOLIDAYS   75

8. SHAME ON IKE   86

9. AROONUS THE PAMPERED   96

10. IKE LIKES   107

11. IKE DISLIKES   117

12. HIS OWN LOGIC   126

13. THE INDIVIDUAL   137

14. IKUS   152

To Dave and Brian

Here Is Your Poodle Puppy

CHAPTER ONE

A FEMALE VISITOR IN OUR HOME is very apt to be scolded if she puts her handbag on a chair, table, or the floor. Things like handbags should be put way—not left lying about the house in a haphazard manner. The fact that visitors cannot avail themselves of this family's storage facilities is a point not completely clear to the one doing the reprimanding.

Just who is this uncouth one? Who would behave in such a way? Who would embarrass us as well as female guests? Dave, my husband? No. Brian, our teen-age son? No. Would I? No.

The answer is the fourth member of our family...a dog.

A dog that answers to a variety of names:

Roony.

Roonoo.

Ikus.

P.Q.R.S.

Aroonus.

Ikus P.Q.R.S. Aroonus.

And, of course, there's *Ike*... which is really his name.

Ike is a black Standard Poodle. A Poodle ... which means that he belongs not to the ordinary canine world, but to that of the Poodle. This is not to say Poodles are better or any more desirable than other dogs. It means only that there is a vast difference between them.

Once we saw a movie about a Poodle that literally ruled his mistress's life, to what at the time we considered a ridiculous degree. This was when our experiences with canines had been limited to Cocker Spaniels, Dalmatians, and Beagles.

This was before we owned a Poodle....

Open your home and your heart to a Poodle and you're in for quite a surprise. You'll discover you've acquired a highly intelligent, many-faceted friend whose very existence is dependent upon your love. You are observed, cataloged, questioned. Your moods are signals to him for his own behavior. He submerges his personality to yours; yet at the same time he remains a unique personality. He is never servile.

A Poodle requires an enormous amount of attention. Grooming alone eats up the hours. He accepts the time spent on such care and responds with love.

He lives for you. It's an obvious joy to him just to be with you. You are his world. You are never secondary to anything like a rabbit chase. But if it should please you to see that he has a rabbit to chase, then he will derive pleasure also.

Completely people-centered, a Poodle is at his best living with people, for people, as nearly as possible the way people do.

And Ike is no exception. Every inch of him is Poodle – and then some. He is comical, aloof, haughty, jealous, playful, demanding....

And lovable.

From the first he was lovable.

On our appointment calendar, under September 6, these words were written: "*Dog* born." The *dog* was to be a gift to us from friends whose only concern was to find the right home for their pick of the litter. A few weeks later, from the litter their Pepe had sired, they chose a male as payment.

And we chose the name *Ike* for our future gift. We didn't want a pretentious name; we didn't want the usual French appellation. Something short, and simple. That's what we wanted. Why? I suppose so that we could turn the short, simple *Ike* into a showy, foreign-sounding name.

Seven weeks after birth, Ike was ready for a home, and we were ready for Ike. Or at least we thought we were. As ready as any family could ever be for Ikus P.Q.R.S. Aroonus. We saw him the first time on a Thursday evening when our friends brought Ike to our home in Southern California. "Here is your Poodle puppy," they said.

We greeted Ike outdoors. He puddled. I secretly questioned his lineage because he looked more like a Cocker Spaniel than a

Poodle. But he *was* a Poodle puppy, the puppy we three had been waiting for. He was the size of two big fists full of kinky black fur flattened into a sturdy box shape. He waddled into the house — still a little stiff from the long automobile ride — and promptly puddled on the rug. Then after eating a big bowl of food he wandered around to make a leisurely survey. He returned to his eating spot to lap up a sizable drink from his water bowl. Another puddle (we were learning, though; we almost got him outdoors in time).

From time to time Ike would look us over and cock his head to one side at the sound of our voices. No fawning, frightened puppy was this one, with such a proprietary air. He wasn't, even during the first few minutes, a stranger. It was almost as if he had watched us from a distance, prior to our meeting, and had already decided we would pass inspection. I wonder ... was it more a case of Poodle taking a family than family taking Poodle?

Unconsciously we began to set all kinds of patterns. If ever I should be asked for one bit of advice to a new Poodle owner, it would be this: *Think twice before you do anything for the Poodle, to him, or with him.* Some act that's now insignificant may haunt the household if it's repeated day in and day out for the rest of the Poodle's life. An enigma of dogdom is what he is. He can be completely adaptable in one situation – and yet in another, one time is all it takes to make an almost irrefutable habit. If you put the puppy to bed at ten o'clock he may always demand a ten o'clock bedtime. And don't presume he'll not know when it's ten o'clock.

True, some of the habits we were helping Ike to form were good ones. Some were questionable. And some, although we couldn't know it at the time, were more like traps for the future. Regardless, some of them were unavoidable.

... Like the second day. You might say it was Poodle open house at the Lusks'. California is Poodle Country, and our neighborhood was filled with Poodle People, all anxious to see the new puppy. Ike was the showpiece. He knew it and gloried in this attention. He used to the nth degree that magic all puppies have – the power to charm children. And sometime during the day every child in our neighborhood met Ike, stroked him, and talked to him. Not only the children, but mothers of the children came also. Ike had reserved enough charm for the mothers. Because our yard wasn't completely fenced in, even the neighborhood Poodles inspected with considerable sniffing the new addition at our house. Especially interested was Abernathy, the Miniature Poodle that lived next door. Aby, a white powder puff with substance, was to be Ike's favorite playmate while we lived in California.

Other friends came to call. One brought a gift to Ike – a quilt, a pad for Ike's bed. She held him on the small floral quilt in her lap, later put the pad on the floor and called Ike to it.

Think twice before you do anything for the Poodle, to him, or with him. A gift of cloth. Was this the start of Ike's passion for rags? Is this why he loves to have gifts brought to him?

And did all the interest in him that day – that unofficial open house – create an impression that people-homage would be a thing permanently due him? Ever since, the doorbell's sound hits Ike with the impact of a fire bell.

Action. Bustle and flurry. Commotion. *That's the doorbell! Get moving. Get to the door. Bark. Company's here. Run in circles. Bark. People! Bark some more. Hope they'll play with me. Yelp. Run round and round. Bark. Boy, oh boy, oh boy. Jump on door. People. People. People.*

Adult friends. Children. Neighbor Poodles. His family. This was the way Ike's world was populated those first few days. All of these at various times.

Sometimes...just one person. Dave and Brian left each weekday for work and school, respectively. I didn't leave. I stayed at

home. I stayed with Ike. I was the faithful one with my presence.

A new puppy in the house is a little like a baby...the four feedings a day...the cleaning up...the constant watching...the attention necessary for safety and health. I was the member of the family who most often tended Ike. Because of availability it fell to my lot to serve. And especially during the housebreaking time, I kept Ike at my side constantly. Even after puddling was unlikely, I continued to keep him close—just in case...a *temporary* precaution. But not in Ike's mind. This was the way it would always be. Now was his training time, and he caught on fast. Always at my side whenever possible.

I have heard that a Poodle attaches himself more closely to one member of a family than to the others. If interpretation means to stay physically close to that one member, then in our family it is I. However, I sincerely believe he loves us all equally and that when he chooses my company in lieu of Dave's or Brian's, it's because of that propinquity of long ago. I have always liked to have Ike by my side. I like it very much. I would not be truthful if I said otherwise. If it didn't please me, why would I want a dog in the first place?

I became *Mommer* to Ike.

This mutilation of *Mama* originated with Brian. It began as a joke, and it stuck. In speaking to Ike about me, what name could Brian have used? Martha? It's never quite natural for a child to use a parent's given name. Brian calls me Mom. It would have been even more unnatural for him to share the *Mom* with Ike. So wrong at first, in time—as with all names—Mommer seemed right.

Then, of course, Dave became *Popper.* It was inevitable.

Because we have a penchant for names, *Ike* gradually was expanded to *Ikus P.Q.R.S. Aroonus.* No particular reason. Dave started it with the *Aroonus.* The remainder just fell into place, letter by letter. The nicknames like Roonoo came later.

Everything should have a name of its own, even an unimaginative one. Ike's very first toy was a plain, gray rubber mouse, and the name bestowed upon it was simply *Mouse.* After the first encounter, when Ike promptly nipped off the last inch of Mouse's gray tail, Ike showed nothing but gentleness with this toy. Even though Mouse was to share the spotlight with many other toys—another rodent named Toothy, a big, bucktoothed, stylized mouse; Benny, a plastic bee; Gulliver, a bright red-and-black ladybug—Mouse was always given more consideration than the others. For a Poodle's toy, Mouse lasted a long time and later shared with Ike one special occasion.

Ike learned Mouse's name promptly. We would say, "Ike, get Mouse." And he would. But gently.

More important, Ike learned his own name quickly...on the second or third day.

And not only his name. During those first few days, when not napping, he was in a constant state of discovery. There were all the things he could do, and the many more he couldn't do. He explored his new world, moving about in a way that was a mixture of clumsiness and poise. He became familiar with—by virtue of sight and smell—the bottom six inches of each piece of furniture; he found all electrical cords in the house and tasted some of them; he searched out crumbs, bits of a string, and fuzz on the floors; with puppy teeth sharp as needles, he examined the texture of the rug edges; he investigated human feet, and the odd covers we put on those feet.

And hands.

Ike learned about human hands, about the dexterity of them, the disapproval they could express, the love they could convey, their part in the joy of play. And it was hands that served food and water.

He listened to human voices and began to learn about communication.

As people do, Ike discovered the entertainment value of television when that first Sunday night he saw Lassie. With dark, almond eyes he watched the screen at least five minutes, watched Lassie bound through the woods; he cocked his head from side to side, twitching his ears when Lassie barked.

Already we thought Ike was special. He had an unusual charm, the canine equivalent of charisma. Before the first week was out, I think Ike had at least one more person thinking as we.

His world broadened a little more — to add a new friend.

"This puppy has the cutest face in town," said the veterinarian as he took Ike up into his arms, against his chest. Ike lifted his head and licked the doctor in the face. I think were I a dog I'd have the theory that a bit of face-licking is the ultimate test for human beings. And had I been Ike that day, the vet would have passed with high honors. Evidently Ike felt the same way. He must have noticed the vet's complete absence of flinching, and he couldn't have missed the vet's gentle pat after Ike's display of affection. Some veterinarians practice in an aloof, detached fashion. Others are gentle, warm and genuine animal lovers. This man belonged to the latter group.

An examination was next.

"Ike," the doctor said at one point. Ike jerked his head around and looked the vet squarely in the eyes.

"He already knows his name is Ike." The vet smiled. "That's for sure."

Now it was time for a puppy injection. Ike reacted to the prick of the hypodermic needle. He yelped. Again the vet lifted Ike, put him to a shoulder, and talked soothingly. Ike snuggled against him for a moment, then sought this time an ear to lick.

"Forgiven me for the pain, haven't you fella?"

One of the things the vet told me during that first visit was, "Just remember this—all in the world Ike wants is to please you." (I wish Ike had listened very closely to this, because there have been many times I've doubted he was trying specifically to *please* us.)

The vet pleased Ike, and Ike in his own way tried to please the vet.

The second time we pulled up in front of the vet's office Ike knew where he was. He was happy all over, to the tip of a wiggling tail.

He knew and was happy the third time . . . the fourth . . . the fifth . . . the sixth . . . the seventh . . . and on and on. . . . The series of three injections for distemper, hepatitis, and leptospirosis; rabies shot; treatment for ears (Ike has always been plagued with ear canker); dental work (yes, dental work—a stubborn puppy tooth had to be extracted); a worming visit and overnight hospitalization; a series of treatments for foot fungus.

Then, too, there were the weekends and one vacation when Ike was boarded there.

Ike never does anything halfway. Even his emotions are unrestrained and overt. The first few times he went to the veterinarian's office he was happy. After that, the happiness was expanded to exuberance. Each time he made a grand entrance, to make certain everyone knew Ikus P.Q.R.S. Aroonus had arrived.

Once inside the lobby, he walked on his hind feet, twisting and dancing. He'd always go up to the reception window barking.

Hello, hello, hello, his barks clearly said.

"Why, hello, Ike," the receptionist usually said. He expected an answer. If the receptionist were on the phone, or busy, and didn't acknowledge his greeting, Ike continued to bark — until she did say something to him. He has always had the idea that all persons should enjoy conversing with him.

Once convinced that the receptionist knew he was there for his appointment, Ike made the rounds to meet all the human beings and all the four-footed creatures in the lobby. Still on his hind feet he commanded their attention.

The vet told me one time that Ike *talked* to them constantly when being boarded or held over for treatment. The doctor and his staff stopped by Ike's run for a chat many times each day.

Is it no surprise then, that Ike enjoyed being a patient and boarder at this office?

It was not the only place, however, where he received preferential treatment.

His world was still broadening. Other than the veterinarian, his canine playmate Abernathy, his human friends, and his family, there was still another friend of great importance to him during his puppyhood.

The Lady

CHAPTER TWO

WE DISCUSSED IT MANY TIMES. We were so certain. We'd never change.

We wouldn't clip a Poodle.

We wouldn't fall into that silly grooming trap. We'd be individualists.

No sissy, effeminate, perfumed, bow-bedecked male Poodle for us.

Ike would remain natural looking.

"A Poodle is a dog, just an ordinary dog. It's absurd to clip him and try to make him into something he isn't — into something fancy." This is what we said soon after we got Ike. We didn't realize we had on our hands the most energetic hair factory imaginable.

Neither did we know the most obvious of Poodle truths: *A Poodle and grooming are synonymous.*

10

There couldn't possibly be any baldness — or even sparse coats — in Ike's ancestry. He grew fast physically. But his coat grew faster; in a short time a great mass of curly black fur completely covered him. When he was a few months old, Ikus P.Q.R.S. Aroonus looked like a miniature black bear . . . maybe he was even more hirsute than the average ursine character.

But we wouldn't clip him. Brush him regularly, as the vet had instructed? Yes. But we wouldn't clip. . . .

"It's your choice," said the vet. But, he explained, it was necessary to remove some of the hair in three areas even on an unclipped Poodle.

The hair shouldn't grow long around the eyes. Why? Possible infection.

The same reason for plucking all hair from inside the ears. Left untended, the ear canal of a Poodle looks as if it's plugged with a wad of cottony hair.

Third, the hair must be removed from between the toes and pads. If not, the feet become sore — maybe infected — and the walk can be affected.

A question was brought to mind. Were we being individualistic when we chose not to clip Ike? Or were we being a bit stubborn?

Once we began to scissor around the eyes and the feet, to pluck ear hair, and other things . . . like cutting toenails, had we not already because of necessity succumbed to that *grooming trap*, as we had labeled it? Had we not already gone halfway? Would there be much difference if we went all the way?

"Have Ike clipped," everyone in Poodle Country was telling us. "You simply *must* get Ike clipped." "His coat will be ruined if you don't." "It's so much easier to teach them grooming manners when they're puppies." "Sooner or later you'll do it; why wait?" "An unclipped Poodle isn't a Poodle."

Protest on our part gradually became reluctant acceptance. In the manner of persons in the process of changing their minds, we were saying, "Maybe," instead of an emphatic "No."

To ease into acceptance we said, "Just a puppy clip." All we'd ever want for Ike would be a puppy clip. Never a more complicated clip. "Even when he's full-grown we'll have only his face, feet, and tail clipped close."

He was six months old, our little dancing bear cub, when he received a somewhat delayed right, when he was finally introduced to full Poodle heritage. He had an appointment at a Poodle grooming salon. The quoted fee was almost ten dollars. *That much to have a puppy clipped?* It was becoming evident as time went on that the price of Poodle ownership was enough to shake the foundation of our budget structure. And to think that some Poodles went to salons frequently.

Ike's appointment was with a salon highly recommended by the Poodle People. "Ike will just love it—because they adore Poodles there." "It's the best salon in the area." "Complete service, too." Including pickup and delivery. Ike's pickup time was to be at 8:30 A.M.

Several times before eight-thirty I told Ike—"A lady will be here."

He understood that *something* was to happen. But he didn't know what it would be—until promptly at half past eight, the doorbell rang. Ike began to bark and run round me. We went to the door.

There she stood. *The Lady.* All pink and white and soft.

I liked her, too. But Ike thought she had been created for him alone, this white-haired lady who wore a strong but pleasant perfume for human noses (perhaps insurance against a doggy scent) and a much more interesting one for Ike's nose. No person can be secretive about recent associations with dogs to another dog. Ike must have surmised that anyone who knew so many dogs must be marvelous. He danced round and round her, yapping and trying to reach her face with his wet strawberry tongue.

"No! Ike, no," I commanded. To no avail. Ike no longer saw or heard me.

At last he reached her face. She didn't seem to mind. "Such a fine boy," she said. "Big old pretty boy."

Several times—when he'd cease the wild gyrations briefly—she'd pat him on the head. She shushed me when I apologized for Ike's behavior.

As they were leaving, I told The Lady, "I hope it won't be too bad—I hope he won't ruin your day—"

"Now you just don't worry," she said. "We handle lots of first-timers. Ike's an excited little boy—he'll settle down. We'll get along just fine."

They went down the walk, Ike leaping round The Lady. He was on his leash, but without it I think he would have stayed with her.

Off they drove, in the Poodle-equipped van, off to that canine domain where The Lady and another woman reigned. A world of clippers, snippers, shampoo, rinses, hair dryers, perfume, sprays, polishes, conditioners. A world of the affluent Poodle—but not necessarily affluent masters. A world envied by women who make

only limited excursions to beauty salons. A world of a chorus of
Poodle yaps, each dog vying for the lion's share of attention. A
world where groomers with almost magical powers train their
charges. A world where raunchy-looking animals enter—and beautiful, elegant creatures exit. A world with which we had been so
sure we'd have no connection. But, of course, we were doing only

what was *necessary*. A puppy clip. That's all. At the most, we'd
send Ike for this clip a couple of times a year.

    Late that afternoon The Lady telephoned. "Just checking to see
if you're in. I'm ready to bring your baby home."

    When Ike was returned, he was calm and tired. His weariness
was equivalent to that of a daylong hunting trip, but his appearance
was unmistakably that of a day of grooming.

    We could see Ike's face again, for the first time since he was very
small, but it was no longer the flat face of a puppy. Where there had
been a lump of fur, there was now a muzzle and a moustache. His
shaved tail sported a pompon on the tip. And now with clipping, his
feet were freed for the expression that only Poodle feet have. His
coat—only lightly scissored—was soft, poufed, and clean; and he
smelled like the perfume counter in a department store. On each
ear was a bright, red ribbon bow which our son Brian removed as
soon as The Lady left. (About two things Brian was—and still is—
adamant. No ribbons, and no jeweled collar.)

    This day was an important one. Ike had been clipped. He was

now a full-fledged Poodle. And he had found out there are persons in the world like The Lady.

He didn't forget her.

Far from it.

The morning of the next clip date, more or less to test his memory, I said to Ike, "The Lady will be here."

The Lady? With a jerk he turned to face me. He stared, as if he were trying to summon a mental replay to be certain he had not imagined my words.

I said it again. "The Lady will be here."

That cinched it. He *had* heard correctly. He ran round and round, barking all the while. *The Lady is coming! The Lady is coming!*

Luckily it was time for her to arrive. I went with Ike to a front window, and we saw the van pull up. The Lady got out. Ike's tail was going like a frenzied metronome.

It was like the first meeting — same jubilant, slurping welcome by Ike. He had no curbs whatsoever when he displayed his fondness for The Lady.

Same soft-spoken words from The Lady. Once again she patted him when he'd be still long enough. "Ike's a doll," she said, more to him than me.

What a testimonial to Ike. The Lady could say this after having had Ike for an entire day, after going through the grooming intricacies with a complete novice? She could say this before the second appointment with a wild one like Ike?

We had removed all individualistic pretense by the time of the second clipping. We were Poodle People now. No longer did we talk about *only a puppy clip.* There was a simple explanation: Dave and I had decided we liked clipped Poodles. Brian was the only holdout, but we managed a compromise: no jeweled collar or ribbons, but we'd go all the way with clipping.

All the way...we were Poodle People.

"We don't want the puppy clip this time—" I said to The Lady. "Put him in the clip you think best suits him."

"That's easy," she said without a pause. "He's built for the Town and Country Clip."

Then the Town and Country it would be.

All the way...the orders were given.

This second day with The Lady brought the big transformation. That afternoon when she brought Ike home Brian and I, anxious to see how Ike looked, were at the window. The Lady got Ike out of the van, and they started up the walk.

We had gone all the way...what had we done? This couldn't be our Ike coming up the walk. He barked, his way of telling us, *Hey everyone, I'm home.* Then we knew, in spite of the change the Town and Country Clip had wrought, it was indeed our Ike. His legs were left full, but his body was clipped close. Instead of ap-

pearing plump—the effect of all that fur around his middle—he now looked long and lean.

Before The Lady and Ike reached the door, Brian said, "I don't like it."

Right then I didn't either. It was too new. "Let's give it time," I said. "We're not used to it yet."

There remained one grooming alteration.

The next time I asked The Lady, "Can we get rid of Ike's moustache?"

A constant nuisance—that's what his moustache had been. He used it as a scoop for food and water, and consequently it was always dirty, or wet, or both.

The Lady answered, "I personally favor the clean jaw line—if the Poodle can wear it. Let's see about old Ike boy." Ike was on his hind feet, prancing round her. She grasped his muzzle firmly in her hand and held his moustache flat to examine his jaw. "He'll look fine without it. Just fine."

And he did. Stripped of his moustache, his muzzle was long and lean to match his body. I think Ike was especially happy to be rid of it, because his *Hey, everyone, I'm home* barks were a little louder than before.

"Doesn't he look aristocratic with a clean jaw?" The Lady asked. "He even *feels* different."

He probably did feel different. But it was due only in part to a muzzle sans moustache.

It was about this time we began to notice the effect of grooming on Ike's personality. For a few days after an appointment with The Lady he'd take enormous pride in his physical transformation. Leaving a waft of Poodle perfume behind him he'd strut through the house as if he found narcissistic pleasure in looking so handsome. During this post-grooming time his actions were more deliberate than usual...such as the dainty cupping and feline-like handling of his front feet.

We could say something like "Ike's such a pretty boy," and his swaggering would shift to the highest gear. Perhaps in his mind The Lady's talent and his willingness to be made attractive were an unbeatable combination.

The Lady's influence was certainly evident on *the box*. On the patio, protected from the weather, was a storage box in which we kept small garden tools and charcoal briquets. The box was the right height on which to put Ike when we cleaned his muddy feet before letting him come back into the house. Heavy California dews made a doggie foot-cleaning station a necessity.

Also, we brushed Ike on the box. He has always enjoyed being brushed. Poodles like attention — which to them is a form of loving. Brushing is attention. After meeting The Lady, Ike's grooming discipline improved... "Hold" and he would... "Sit" and he would.... Of course, responses to commands were tempered with limited puppy endurance.

Activity on the box spawned closer human-canine understanding. It spawned talk.

...Talk about the mockingbird always there on the utility pole at the back of the yard. The bird would call — a trill, a caw, or some harsh chatter. With a grayish flutter it would rise up a foot or so, then realight on the pole.

"Is that Ike's bird?" we began to ask.

Ike would look up at the bird and whine. Gradually any mockingbird became known as Ike's bird.

...Talk about such things as bones, balls, Mouse. And Toothy. And Benny. And Gulliver. The handsomeness of Ike. The various activities of human neighbors as they went about their gardening and outdoor living.

...Talk about the old Siamese cat — a very favorite conversation topic on the box.

To offset the lack of fence, my husband Dave put a long chain on a swivel stake in the yard for Ike. The chain afforded Ike a certain amount of freedom for somewhat brief periods of outdoor time. The length of Ike's chain was no secret to the Siamese cat. Contemptuously flipping her tail back and forth, she'd amble across our yard — just barely out of Ike's reach. What greater blow to a dog's dignity could there be? We used to tell him, "Someday, Ike, we'll unhook your chain and retribution will be yours."

...Talk about Abernathy. Often Aby would come to visit during Ike's brushing session, and he'd wait around for a frolic with Ike

later. Aby, being a Poodle, too, knew all about grooming, all about brushing and clipping. Aby also knew The Lady. Perhaps he and Ike talked to each other about her. When Aby had been groomed and was once again clean and white, he'd run to our yard and bark for Ike to come out. Likewise, when Ike had been with The Lady and was once again clean and black, he would call Aby: *Come see what The Lady did to me.*

We didn't dare say "The Lady" in Ike's hearing unless we were waiting for a pickup and she was already coming up the walk. When Ike heard the words "The Lady" he was ready to go with her immediately.

After the third clipping we set up a standing appointment. *Standing appointment.* For the dog that would be professionally groomed maybe twice a year. His appointments were six weeks apart, and about the fifth week he would have that ursine look again.

One clip day I had hidden Ike's leash in a little cabinet by the front door, in readiness for The Lady's arrival. I was in the kitchen washing breakfast dishes when I heard a scratching noise. It was Ike. By combining a little Bloodhound with Poodle, he had located his leash and was trying to claw open the cabinet door. When I walked up, he started to bark and run in circles. He'd make a slight pause at the front door during each circle to tell me he knew he was going. Then, as if it were all planned, he ceased his circle running and made a leap into a chair—skidding it a foot or so, almost into the front window. He looked out, toward the street. Then he jumped down. Then up into the chair again. From the chair to the floor. From the floor to the chair. Quick surveys of the street.

There was no doubt. He was looking for The Lady. He knew, because of the leash by the door...the time of day...and maybe canine intuition.

I spent a hectic ten minutes or so trying to calm him, during which time I told myself I'd never again try to hide his leash. Thank goodness, The Lady was prompt, as was her custom.

I could understand Ike's anxiousness to go with her. Once she told me, "Ike doesn't like to have his topknot dried unless I hold him in my lap."

Sometimes Ike tried to assist The Lady by doing his own clipping. He chewed off the hair on the bottom of his ears. Just about the time the feathering would begin to grow out, Barber Ike would go to work again. I asked the vet about it. His answer was: "Ike is hyperactive. This is just something to do when he gets bored."

How do you prevent boredom for a Poodle that has attention literally lavished upon him?

Accomplished though she was, there was nothing The Lady could do, short of supplying ear wigs, to offset Ike's barbering.

If before an appointment Ike looked like a bear, he certainly did not after he was clipped. Afterward, he resembled a praying mantis. At least he did during (if dogs are allowed such a human development) his awkward stage—before he matured and filled out. This was a time when physical characteristics that would later look natural now were out of proportion. His body seemed too long, too lean. So did his neck—and his tail. His topknot wouldn't stand erect; most of the time it looked like a mushroom that had been stepped on. Because Ike kept the feathering sheared off, his ears were much too short for balance.

His overall awkward appearance was emphasized by his feet. Big feet. Feet that looked as if they should be on a dog three times Ike's size. The vet laughed when he noticed how they had grown. "Either he'll grow to these big feet, or he'll be just a good old boy."

The vet also had a description of Ike's front teeth. "They look like he's been opening bottle caps with them."

Gradually his teeth straightened up. Now they're just slightly crooked. It's all right, though. I doubt if perfect teeth would look good on Ike.

He did grow to his feet. And his body is now in proportion. He is sleek and graceful. Maturity banished awkwardness — in this instance proving things *bad* are sometimes short-lived.

But by the same token some things *good* are not permanent.

When Ike was eighteen months old, we were transferred to Dallas, Texas.

No longer could *The Lady* mean a clip date.

Ike still remembered her long after the last time he saw her. We could say "The Lady" in his hearing, and he would tense up, listening intently — perhaps for the sound of the Poodle van, or the doorbell announcing her arrival, or her voice. He would whine.

I believe he thought of her when he was brushed and bathed... when he was fluff-dried... when he stood at attention for hours as he was combed and clipped, combed and clipped, combed and clipped...when his toenails were trimmed and filed...when those hands grooming him were not as professional as The Lady's.

Dave and I thought of The Lady, too. Gratefully. Appreciatively. She made our study and practice go much smoother. She had taught Ike which foot is clipped first . . . when to lie down . . . when to sit . . . when to stand. Ike, in turn, taught us.

You see, we began to groom Ike when we moved to Dallas.

CHAPTER THREE

WHAT IS THE GREATEST MEASURE of a natural clown? Resourcefulness. If there isn't an obvious vehicle for jocundity, he invents one. . . .

One day Ike walked up to a closet, used a foot to open the door, then sat down and barked because the door was open. It didn't matter to him that I had seen the entire incident; if anything, that added substance to the performance. The door was open — that was an indisputable fact — regardless of the *how* and *why*, and Ike wanted me to close it. He continued to bark indignantly until I finally shut the door.

Why shouldn't Ike do something funny to make me notice him when my interest is too long, in his opinion, on other things?

From the very beginning of his life with us he has been the cynosure of the Lusk household. He has known the infectiousness, also, of being the center of attention with friends . . . the veterinarian . . . The Lady. It would seem logical that Ike would want to be more than a recipient of all this consideration. Would he not want to entertain in return?

He does. He wants to entertain. Definitely.

The whole world is not Ike's stage. He doesn't need such a large one. A small stage does very well, one about the size of his personal domain. His own little theater. It's perfect. Everything is there, from props to a sympathetic audience. A flexible schedule with no specific curtain times. Performances are apt to be any time, day or night.

Ike relishes being the star of his own little theater. His many moods, many faces, his awareness of various nuances—all help to make him a good actor. He can play any role, but the one that delights him the most—the one he plays with the greatest gusto—is that of a clown.

A clown. A clown. Clown Ike. He has a fundamental theory—if it's in fun it isn't wrong. That includes taking things from us, an act that were it not under the guise of entertainment very possibly could be labeled stealing.

In the yard...when we're gardening and have amassed a neat pile of weeds, Ike sneaks up, grabs a bundle of weeds in his mouth and runs. If we don't participate as an appreciative audience should, the act ends a few feet away. He drops his *haul* and goes on about his business of bug-sniffing and animal-people-bird patroling. But if we participate as we're expected to do, then the fun begins. We yell something like "Stop—thief!" and Ike runs round and round with calculated speed, head held high. Ah, delicious detection. He's caught in the act with weeds spilling out of his mouth, but surrender is out of the question.

In the house, too, Ike appropriates our possessions—things of a more personal nature than weeds. His cache is his own bed, and we're never surprised at the multitude of articles we find there. It might be a sock, an undershirt, a glove, a small throw pillow, a dish towel, a straw basket, a magazine, a belt, a scarf, a letter, a shoe.

It might even be one of his own towels we find in his bed. Then, of course, it can't be misappropriation if the item belongs to him. But it's a way of teasing. When it's raining, we don't always hang up Ike's towel after drying his feet...a bad habit, we'll admit. It started in California. Why hang it up when it would be used again shortly? was our excuse. By the back door it was handy; we could pick it up on our way to the box. It was also handy for Clown Ike.

Not long ago he did it again. He walked by the back door, saw his towel lying there, picked it up and took it to his bed. I replaced the towel, by the door. As I turned away, he dashed back, snatched up the towel again and returned it to his bed. I replaced it again. Ike took it to his bed again. It went on as long as *I* thought it was funny.

Weeds, household items, clothing, damp foot towels . . . the simple things are stage props to Ike. Common things, like the house fly.

Fly-fighting started the first time he saw a fly swatted. Did the idea strike a responsive chord in his hunter's heart? Or did the solid whack of the swatter excite him? At any rate, now fly-fighting is a big show. When we say "I'll get it," that's Ike cue.

He yelps, runs, jumps at the wall, the table, the chair, the floor, wherever the fly is.

In fact, there doesn't even have to be a fly.

Just the words, "I'll get it."

The usual weapon with which one hunts flies isn't necessary either. A magazine, a section of newspaper, even a bare hand — any one of these is acceptable for real or imaginary flies.

Fly-fighting is a wild, intense act. It's difficult to keep from laughing even though the performance has been repeated many, many times. It's like applause to Ike when we laugh because it's laughter that's in fun. Dogs know intuitively whether laughter is cruel or filled with merriment.

His antics with his ball bring the merry kind of laughter and put Ike center stage. He runs, with his ball in his mouth. He pitches the ball. Then while running with a silly, too-fast, exaggerated gait he scoops up the ball as he circles round — without breaking stride.

To keep momentum, he'll make the second pass if he misses the ball on the first.

There's no more valuable stage prop than a ball. Ike learned this when he was a few months old....

Quite accidentally (I think), he pushed his ball under a bookcase. He tried but couldn't reach it with a paw. There was only one action to take — bark. That's Ike's answer to any dilemma — bark for his people to come to his aid. We did. That made it worth a repeat. Again he pushed the ball under the bookcase, then barked unceasingly until we retrieved it.

Then for a time, almost nightly, he put on the same act. We co-operated and did our part. And we laughed. It was funny to watch him take his ball to the bookcase, and with a foot or his nose push it out of sight. Next would come that feigned look of surprise because his ball was beyond recovery. There he'd be, chest on the floor, rear up in the air, tail straight up waving a distress signal, while he barked repeatedly.

It's something he has never forgotten. He must think it's too juvenile to use often, but occasionally he shoves his ball under the bookcase. It's a good way to get our attention and a few laughs.

Just one person can be an audience. And center stage for a little favorite in his repertoire is in Dave's and my bathroom, where there are two throw rugs of unequal size on the floor. It goes like this: First, a quick check to see if a pair of eyes are on him, then he begins to dig furiously on the larger rug while all hunched up like a Beagle escaping under a fence.

"No! No! No!" He doesn't look up; he completely ignores the commands to stop. He quits when the digging is finished; how *he* knows when, I don't know, but there is a definite time involved. When the rug is heaped into the exact small brown mountain that Ike wants, he proceeds to the other rug and flops down.

There could be reasons like frustration, or thwarted bone-excavating, or some unknown psychological need to explain Ike's digging on the bathroom rug, but I think it might be nothing more than the conduct of a clown. It's an amusing little act...but one that in entertainment value doesn't come up to his *growling* routine.

A farce allows great latitude in credibility. The freedom of make-believe. Ike understands make-believe, knows how to use it; never it is more evident than when he *growls*. Our son Brian and Ike perfected this routine, and there is a rapport between the two of them as Brian leads Ike into and through the act. (It is definitely a Brian-Ike show. It never quite comes off for Dave and me; we're better as the audience.)

It's difficult to believe it's only an act. If Ike isn't ready for the curtain call, Brian can coax him into the act with nudges and commands — "Growl. Growl, Ike." However, if the act is begun when Ike is relaxing or asleep, there is very little coaxing needed.

Once the routine is underway, Ike is a manifestation of fury. Mock fury.

What viciousness. What abominable horror. Deep throaty growls. Lips peeled back. Fangs bared. Brian touches him, runs his hands under Ike for the lift, and the growls intensify and become those of a truculent beast of the wild.

The audience snickers, and the magic of the stage envelopes Ike completely. If there's any of his acting ability not already in use, he plunges that last vestige into his performance. He *is* the beast and not the actor.

Brian picks him up. The viciousness subsides. Ike snuggles up against Brian, maybe settles down for a quick little nap. It must be remembered that he is with someone he knows and loves. With a stranger there would be no *acting* involved.

There is a variation of the growling farce. If we're all sitting in the den, and Brian decides to pick Ike up, the King's X right may be exercised by Ike. Out of the corner of his eye he sees Brian's approach. Ike snarls and gets set to move swiftly. Just as Brian reaches out, Ike skitters past, his hindquarters brushing past Brian's open hands. Ike leaps into a chair, by Dave or me . . . this is the King's X territory. This is where Ike seeks asylum. Brian cannot reach him, because Brian honors the respite. Once settled by Dave or me, the look Ike gives Brian is that of a child who, with a sing-song victory chant, chides a playmate who lost the game.

People reaction — audience response — is a measuring stick. I think that explains why Ike puts so much emoting into his growling routine.

HOWEVER, NOT ALL OF HIS comedial behavior is as amusing to his audience as it is to Ike himself.

From the outset of the relationship between Ike and his people there were the usual puppy mishaps — puddles, chewed up socks and the like, but Ike, being Ike, added his own brand of humor.

The utility room became our puppy's bedroom. Between it and the kitchen Dave installed a half door. Now Ike had a place of his own and privacy. We, too, had privacy, plus peace of mind while we were away from home, knowing that Ike was secured in his own room. Laundry decor I suppose would best describe Ike's quarters. Mixed in with the laundry equipment were Ike's wicker bed and pad, water bowl, food bowl, plastic placemat. And toys...a little ball (the size to go under bookcases), a big beach ball...Mouse... Benny...Gulliver...Toothy. And his house bone.

In his own room was where Ike slept at night. With this custom, we deviated from the ways of most Poodle People. Ike has never slept with Dave and me, nor with Brian.

Long after Ike was housebroken and we were to be away from home, we spread an ample supply of newspapers on the utility room floor. Perhaps we used papers too long, for Ike made use of them. With maddening ingenuity. He always kept in mind a trium-virate of special occasions — Christmas, New Year's Eve, and Hobby Time. He furnished us with excelsior for packing Christmas gifts; confetti for celebrating New Year's Eve; and by dampening the newspaper before shredding it, the material for papier-mâché.

When we finally discontinued the newspapers in his room, how wrong we were to expect Ike to be contented with ordinary pas-times like chewing on his house bone, playing with Mouse and the other toys, or taking a nap now and then. No ordinary activities for Ike. He preferred a different kind of outlet for his energy during those shut-in periods. It was a good time to assist The Lady with his ear barbering. But that was a limited activity. Once the feather-ing was chewed off on both ears that was that — until a new growth came in.

He needed a logical, long-range chewing program. He cast about and found one. His wicker bed. A lot of chewing there. Good for many penned-up stretches.

Our chuckles — the ones Ike surely expected — weren't forthcom-ing as he gradually gnawed off all the sides of his bed. When there was nothing left but a straw pancake, we discarded it. And because of our vexation at the time we didn't replace it with a new one. I made a large pad with removable cover that was actually a small mattress. This we put directly on the floor. He could just get by without a bed. It wasn't until we moved to Texas that he once again had all the sleeping accouterments. We bought him another bed, but not a wicker one — hard plastic this time. So far it has escaped mutilation. Nevertheless, I wouldn't be surprised sometime to find evidence of gnawing. But at this point in Ike's life it wouldn't be puppy teething, or puppy mischief, but mature dog revenge for mistreatment (in his mind) at the hands of his people.

Now beds aren't for gnawing.

But bones are. Both kinds. Yard bones (the real, honest-to-goodness, greasy, too-messy-to-eat-in-the-house, meat shop variety) and house bones (the type bought in pet shops).

Ike's house bone is like an old friend to him, for it's the same one he had when a puppy. Its age testifies to its durability; it's made of a tough, durable synthetic material. Although when new it was shiny and smooth, it is now not only dull and rough but also smaller in size. After all Ike's gnawing on it, it is like a small prickly corn-

cob, studded with thorns. There is no one designated spot for Ike's house bone. He puts it wherever he wants it. We are accustomed to having our decor embellished by canine touches. Most of the time, even a day or so later, Ike remembers exactly where he last placed his house bone, should he desire to chew on it or use it for some other purpose.

Recently Ike and I were alone in the den. I had taken my shoes off. Because I was reading I hadn't been paying particular attention to Ike. Suddenly the doorbell rang.

I jumped up and thrust a foot into a shoe — but not all the way for my toes encountered something hard and rough. I jerked my foot back. Then I picked up my shoe to see what was in it.

It was our little canine jester's house bone.

One day while cleaning in the den, I picked up his house bone and to get it out of my way I put it on a windowsill. Later I heard Ike scratching. I saw him clawing at the windowsill. He seized his bone, and with it in his mouth walked haughtily away. I didn't follow him at the time but later discovered where he had taken his bone.

To Dave's and my bedroom.

To the bed. To the exact middle of the bed. There the bone lay, a symbol of another attempt on the part of Ikus P.Q.R.S. Aroonus to be funny.

Brian for one wasn't always convinced that Ike's clowning is laughable.

When Brian was learning to drive, a few times he practiced while the entire family was in the car. Dave would remain in the front seat with Brian, and I sat in the back with Ike. The moment Brian slid behind the wheel. Ike made a dive toward me and burrowed behind my back. He would try to hide throughout Brian's driving session.

Ike's performance, Brian felt—and rightly so—was entirely out of line.

WHILE HIS COMEDY IS OFTEN a result of the obvious, there are those occasions when Ike is charming because he does *not* try to be funny. It just comes out that way.

Normally a Poodle is a graceful, agile creature—capable of nimble maneuverings that would befit even a cat. To swing the balance from pure grace to buffoonery takes just a hint of another ingredient...it might be slight exaggeration—or emphasis—or repetition. This less-than-perfect grace is amusing to watch.

In California when he'd be on his chain, Clown Ike kept an inventory of the garden debris around him—the twigs, the rose petals, the spent bougainvillea and geranium blooms, an occasional bit of rubbery succulent that had broken off the mother plant. He inspected them all, but the leaves were his chief concern as they blew across the lawn. Those that came to rest within his chain's limit were noted, but that's all.

The leaves that for some reason of aerodynamics were airborne to a greater distance were the most fascinating to Ike.

Suddenly he'd spot a leaf, a crisp one, scurried along by a little gust of wind. He'd make a tentative check. Yes, it was a trifle beyond his reach. Fine, then. This was *the* one. He'd stretch, sometimes from a sitting position, sometimes while lying on his stomach. Stretch...stretch...his right foot extended as far as possible, pawing the air with a wide arc, still short of the leaf by an inch or so.

For any audience available it was an exaggerated heroic attempt, a clown's repetitive effort to surmount obstacles of his own making.

Then he'd bark for people help. *Come out here and get that leaf for me.* More barks. More stretching. More barks.

Get out here fast! Now barks that showed patience was almost gone.

How many times, because of his insistence, I had to walk into the yard, pick up a leaf and give it to Ike. And it had to be that one particular leaf. If I presented the wrong one to him, he wouldn't accept it. He merely barked until I gave him the right one.

Outdoors, Ike played to larger audiences. From their yards, the California Poodle People watched and laughed as Ike tried to catch leaves.

Also, they watched his outdoor walking act. I used to think he walked more on his rear feet than on all fours. When he'd spy Abernathy, or the Siamese cat, Ike's bird, a child, an adult, Ike would stand up and move about in a stilted ballet form, now and then stopping for an instant but still in an upright position. He would remain erect so long it would come as a small shock when he reverted to all fours. Being hooked to his chain made it seem even more a planned, rehearsed performance, almost like a circus act.

But it isn't always for audience appreciation, this *people walk.* On his hind feet he can often see better. And in what place is a good view more important than in the kitchen?

Once, when Ike was a puppy, we had picked up Dave at the office and after arriving home all went to the kitchen. I suppose Ike forgot that earlier he had watched me put dinner in the oven ready to be cooked, because now he walked back and forth on his hind feet, inspecting. He'd look at the counter top, then at me. This particular day there was no visual sign of any meal preparation in sight. I had left out none of the usual cans or packages of food. After a complete perusal he started to bark. *Where is the food?* Still on his hind feet, he was speaking to *me.*

Mommer, aren't you going to feed your family?

Now long after this incident, one evening I had prepared a TV snack. Dave and I were waiting for Brian to come from his room to join us, and in the interim I began to pat Ike. Abruptly he turned away, stood up on his hind feet, and walked over to take a sniffing look at the snack tray I had placed out of his reach.

He looked at me and barked. *No love stuff, please. I'm ready for the snack.*

When Ike isn't trying to be funny—when it just comes out that way—he can be overbearing.

Because Ike has always gone with me into every room in the house, he has likewise claimed the right—if he so desired—to accompany women guests into various rooms.

Including the bathroom.

We try to discourage this, because of an embarrassing incident related to me by a female guest. While Ike was in the bathroom with her he walked up to the room deodorant spray can, nudged it, then looked reprovingly at the guest.

There are some things to which a guest shouldn't be subjected …one of which is to be told to spray by a big, black Poodle playing the droll.

A big, black, male Poodle that has an incorrect concept of his size. In spite of the fact Ike measures nineteen inches at the shoulder and weighs over thirty-five pounds, he thinks he's a little Poodle.

When he and I are waiting in the car, perhaps for Brian at school, he mimics the Toys and Miniatures he sees gamboling about in the other cars. The little Poodles jump into the laps of their people to peer out of the front windows. Ike jumps into my lap to do the same. When he does, I can see nothing but black fur. And I can't breathe because he's pushing hard against me.

I gasp for breath. Then I push Ike back to a position more suited to a Standard. There he stays until he sees another small Poodle in a driver's lap. And it happens often, because North Dallas, like Southern California, is Poodle Country...but more Toy and Miniature Poodle Country. Here Standards are uncommon. In at least every third car or so, it seems there is a frisky little Poodle.

While waiting in the car by himself, several times Ike has stepped on the horn rim. The idea of a Poodle honking the car horn is amusing, but it will be ridiculous if it ever dawns on him that he can summon us.

THERE CAN BE AN ELEMENT of pathos in a clown's performance when the laughter is at the clown's expense.

At times like this...there had been a thunderstorm, and although it had almost subsided, some of the wind remained. There was now a light rain falling. We let Ike out. Just as he got to the middle of the patio, a gust of wind whipped around and overturned a chair. A loud thud. Ike yelped, jumped sideways — away from the sound — and scurried back through the door we held open.

We laughed at his speedy retreat, but we shouldn't have. His tail went between his legs; his ears sagged. His people had let him down, had humiliated him in his time of fear. We couldn't coax him outside for several hours.

It was laughter at Ike's expense, too, one day at the bedroom door. Ike knocked (a paw's light scratching) and my husband let him in. Playfully Dave stepped out into the hall. Ike followed (if Dave were leaving the bedroom then Ike would go with him). Quickly Dave stepped back into the room and closed the door in Ike's face. A moment later Dave opened the door again.

There sat a dejected Ike. Head low, eyes sad. Dave immediately squatted down and gave Ike some people loving.

If there's anything worse than people laughter at the wrong time, it's being put down by a cat.

The old Siamese cat in California had taunted Ike too long. The chain had held him back too many times. The day finally came.

The cat sauntered by, just out of reach as usual. And, as usual, it set Ike off. There was wild yapping and frustrated bouncing and stretching. Dave said, "This is it, boy," and released Ike.

With a warrior's courage and unlimited faith, Ike charged the cat. He met her on the upward slope at the back of the yard, in the patch of ice plant.

It was over quickly.

The experienced old cat halted, hissed, lifted a spread out paw, and ended it with one sharp, swift slap to Ike's face.

Ike is too happy a creature to nurse a wounded pride for any length of time.

BY FAR, MOST OF THE TIME his comedy is gay and refreshing. He has always liked to direct most of his humor to his people.

When he was about four months old, one day while Brian was at school, Ike discovered a photograph of Brian. *That's Brian! That's Brian!* Over and over he looked at the picture, then at me, and barked.

You're such a silly mother. Don't you know that's your own son hanging on the wall? That's what his barks meant.

And with Ikus P.Q.R.S. Aroonus most of the time it's not difficult to figure out the meaning of his *speech.* From puppyhood, regardless of the role being played, he has never underestimated the importance of communication.

CHAPTER FOUR

AT SOME POINT PUPPY IKE must have decided that to be a part of our family he would have to communicate.

But no time had been wasted.

Hadn't it begun that very first night... when he cocked his head to listen to our voices?

It didn't take him long to see that human conversation was like a game of ball—bouncing back and forth, from person to person.

Back and forth. And from family to Ike. From the veterinarian to Ike. From The Lady to Ike. He learned to take part, to be ready when it was his turn. He learned to answer.

Ike always answers.

If he could have one wish granted, it might very well be to speak the words of his people. He has to be content with the word substitutes—the groans, the grunts, the barks; his choice depends on the particular conversation. He doesn't speak in the same manner when flopping down into a comfortable nap position as he does when the discussion is about *going.*

We speak; Ike speaks. It is sharing—between Ike and his people. It is communication.

Ike asks for food. A series of barks.

"Are you hungry?"

One bark. *Yes.*

The food is in hand. "Is this what you want?"

One bark. *Yes.*

"Are you sure?"

Series of barks. *Yes. Yes. Yes.*

Does he think he comes close to our speech? I can say very sternly "Brian!" and Ike barks once—sternly, mimicking my inflection. Or does he know it's his own language but understandable to us, too?

Just as some of our speech is understandable to him.

A great portion of it, because Ike knows the key to communication. He discovered it when he was a puppy: *Awareness of his people and their actions.* The key, Ike found out, was not something learned and then retained forever but that it had to be worked at constantly. That is, if a Poodle wanted to remain absolutely close to his people. And Ike did.

Closeness to people meant learning the human names for everything. Poodle vocabulary—Ike's began with personal nouns. The first one, of course, was his own name. Then came Brian, Popper, Mommer. That was only the start. Abernathy. Mouse, and the other toys—Toothy, Benny, Gulliver. The veterinarian. Ike's bird. Cat. The Lady. And bone. And ball—but with a finer shade of meaning. Little ball, and big ball. Vocabulary training meant that when commanded to go get the big ball, Puppy Ike never returned with the little ball.

Puppy Ike watched and listened and learned, took note of the ways people exchanged ideas, transmitted their thoughts. One people instrument of communication—a thing held in the hand and talked into—caught his attention early.

Ike had discovered the telephone.

The girl in the vet's office used one at her desk. The vet had one, too. And at home his people used two of them. It was one thing to see people use telephones. It was another to relate phones to his own activities.

Around five o'clock each day Dave telephoned for me to come after him, and that call meant a short trip for Ike unless his Mommer let him down. Wouldn't it be less likely that I'd leave Ike home if he recognized that late afternoon call and then begged to go? Of course. So my husband's call became Ike's call. Ike answered it.

This was the only regular daily call we received. This was the only call Ike answered—and only during the period from about 4:30 P.M. until 5:30 P.M. did he answer. A call at three o'clock would get no response from him. Only during Ike's telephone hour.

He answered the only way a young Poodle could. With barks— the first ones sputtered out while running to the telephone. Then there would be a brief cessation of barking, barely time for the human "Hello."

Once again the barking resumed. A loud, deafening sound because he stood so close, right at the telephone. Ike's people were learning, too. We knew we had only that brief, valuable interval at the very first in which to get across vital information without canine interruption. Dave learned to say very quickly something like— "Ten minutes—" or "Ready now—" or "I'll call later—."

Some days, ahead of time—about 4:15 P.M.—I put Ike on his chain in the backyard. He could still hear the phone. He still barked to answer it, but at least he wasn't barking into my ears and into the receiver.

I hated for anyone else to call during Ike's telephone hour. It was impossible to hear, impossible to carry on a normal conversation. I often wondered what an unknowing person thought who called our number expecting a normal answer. "I'm sorry!" I'd yell into the phone, trying to be heard over Ike's noise. "The dog answers the phone this time of day."

Even persons informed ahead were skeptical. One day at the office Dave told a man about Ike's telephone answering.

"You're kidding!"

"It's 4:40 P.M. now. Here's my home number. Dial it."

The man dialed. And Ike answered as usual.

"You're right," the man told Dave. "Your dog does answer the telephone."

Our friends—those who knew Ike—accepted the telephone answering as one of his many eccentricities. One day while lunching with friends, I answered a question with "I can't remember, but I have the information in a book at home."

One of the friends spoke up. "Why not call home and ask Ike to look it up? He answers the phone anyway."

Ike learned about the telephone because of the key to communication...that awareness of his people and their actions.

Constant observation, watching, learning. Oh, how Ike has worked at it. If he hadn't found that key to communication he might still have only a limited puppy vocabulary, might not be so close to his people.

Without the key to communication many peripheral benefits might have been lost to him.

FOR EXAMPLE, THE BENEFITS OF WINDOWS.

Consider the things a Poodle might miss if he didn't comprehend: "Go look out the office window." "Go look out the den window." "Look out the guest room window."

How terrible it would be to look out the den window when the instructions indicated the guest room window. Why a Poodle might miss seeing the milk truck across the street, a cat, a neighbor gardening.

Communication...understanding human language....

When Brian says, "I think I'll go look out my window," how could Ike race Brian and be there first if he didn't know which window Brian meant?

Watch. Listen. Tabulate. Remember. The way to understand the human language.

From the kitchen window one day Brian and I were watching birds at the backyard feeder. Suddenly Brian said, "Look, Mom— there's a bluebird!" Ike heard; he understood, and fulfilling his usual desire to avoid missing anything he ran to us, stood erect and tried to push in to see the bird, too.

"No, Ike," Brian said. "It's too crowded here. Go look out the den window."

Ike reverted to all fours and rushed to the den window.

He barked at the bluebird, an acceptable practice under Ike's own bird laws. But never a bark at Ike's bird.

According to Ike's bird laws, there are two kinds of birds. The first is Ike's bird, and all the others — the second kind — are known simply as bird. He knows them both by name. Bird and Ike's bird. Say "There's Ike's bird," and he looks high, toward a utility pole or line, where a mockingbird usually perches.

Ordinary birds are found much lower.

One time when Ike and I were parked in front of the school I spotted a robin strutting across the lawn, its orange breast jogging up and down with its little fat-man hops. I said, "Ike, there's a bird." Immediately Ike jumped to the car window and looked low. He saw the bird. He barked at it.

Birds aren't the only interesting sights that can be seen from a car window. After we moved to Texas, Ike's vocabulary swelled to include many new creatures that as a strictly city-living Poodle he hadn't the opportunity to see in Southern California. His first country drive here let him see cattle, chickens, and ducks. And horses. The surprised look on Ike's face when he beheld his first horse couldn't have meant anything but that he thought he had found the biggest dog in the world. These strange new Texas animals were not to be met personally — just watched from a window.

Windows are for the study of meteorology, too. In California Ike first began to learn about weather and its effect on the days.

Perhaps the most appreciated were the sunshine days, the balmy fun days when Aby was most likely to bark for Ike to come play.

Perhaps the least appreciated were the smog days...with their bitter, irritating smell and fumes.

And there were the fog days, when from the sea the fog rolled in like a giant whisper.

And, of course, the rain days.

The gentle rain that is most usual in Southern California. The rain that Ike liked to walk in, liked to lift his face to, liked to smell of. The rain that dampened only the top layer of fur.

Conversation about the California rain..."It's raining, Ike." "See the rain?"...Ike understood. He would go to the nearest window to see for himself. In Dallas he learned the same conversation heralded a much more violent rain to watch.

Rain that was preceded and accompanied by gusty, whistling wind that would make spinning tops of Ike's leaves. Wind that would shovel up a batch of those leaves and sail them through the air until they were completely out of sight.

Violent rain and wind. And hail.

That first spring in Texas, after a hailstorm which Ike had watched closely from the den window, he ran to the kitchen door and barked insistently. Now that the odd, thick rain had ceased, it was time to investigate. When Ike went out, he very carefully walked across the layer of frozen ice pellets. He smelled them, even ate a few bites. I wonder if he noticed the similarity between the outdoor variety and the ice which we took from the refrigerator and put into glasses.

There was yet another kind of weather to be found in Texas. Ike was asleep in the den the first time it snowed. Brian awakened him. "Ike! Look out the window! Look at the *snow!*"

Snow? What is snow? Another new word.

This was one of those times when learning is more important than sleep. Ike arose and started to the window, slowly, the languidness of sleep still upon him. About halfway there he looked out and saw the snow. Instant alert. Effects of sleep cast off as he sped to the window. For a minute or so he was silent as he stared at the falling snow. The sparse cover of snow on the ground looked like a giant quilt worn threadbare in spots.

Silence ended. Ike was rendered vocal again. He barked. Again and again he barked. From time to time he'd glance at us. His barking became part bark and part groan. Snow was not a commonplace window view. Snow was worthy of emotion.

Snow...a new word...a new meteorological phenomenon of nature.

Snow...only in winter did snow happen. Only when it was cold.

The first bitter wintry morning after we moved to Dallas, I let Ike out, then back in. When Dave came to breakfast Ike barked at him and ran to the window, then to the door.

"Do you want out?" Dave asked.

No. Ike ran back to the window. Again he barked at Dave.

Some weather acts could be seen — rain, fog, smog, and certainly the hail of the spring storm Ike had watched. But *cold* — this cold weather — couldn't be seen. Ike knew it was there, nevertheless. *Cold* had sent him shivering to the back door earlier. Ike was trying to give Dave a weather forecast.

We point out things to Ike that he should see from the window. He in turn informs us of sights. He has always told us about the happy views — Aby, The Lady, friends, the return of a family member.

Also, Ike with wild barking has always warned us of the questionable views, such as delivery men and strangers.

Window reporting is a form of communication.

COMMUNICATION. What is communication to Ikus P.Q.R.S. Aroonus?

It's a knowledge of individual words.

It's vocabulary. A large one that began with those first puppy words, that initial vocabulary training.

It's knowing the meaning of words like bed, okay, want.

It's knowing breakfast, lunch, dinner, snack, biscuit, cookie, food.

It's knowing walk, dance, heel, come, stay, sit, no, yes, quiet.

And baby, boy, girl, man, woman.

Leash, brush, comb, sweater, ear medicine, spray.

It's knowing the rooms of the house, each one by name — the difference between one bedroom and the next, the difference between foyer and hall.

But communication isn't only individual words. It's also words grouped together. It's understanding sentences:

"Brian will soon be home."

"It's nearly time for Dave."

"Listen — do you hear something?"

"Go look in your bowl."

"Look at TV."

"Put your head down."

"Tell Dave"..."Tell Brian"...or tell a guest.

"Go home, dog!"

Communication is knowing "It's time." Time for what? At night it means bedtime. During the day, it's an alert signal.

It's understanding a question like "Are you ready, Ike?" Ready ...its many shades of meaning...ready to go out?...ready to catch the ball?...ready for guests?

Another question that is open to interpretation by Ike is "What, Ike?" This calls for an immediate answer—a bark. *What?* He finds a *what*—if one isn't right at paw and mind. It takes only a moment to find one. *What* could be food, or water, or a game of ball, or out.

But communication isn't just individual words—or sentences. It's more.

It's learning to recognize important words in the context of his people's conversation. And an important word, perhaps the most important, is the simple two-letter verb *go*. A little word maybe by human measurement, but a big one to Ike. *Go* is a word well worth listening for, even if it's in the middle of a sentence. And once heard, excitement is triggered. Reaction to *go* can be compared to Ike's animation after the doorbell rings. No outright invitation, just the word *go* spoken in a conversation. Only a slim possibility — but Ike is ready. He begs. On his hind feet he dances, jumps, paws at us.

Unless we actually have plans to leave and take Ike with us, we try not to use the word. This is difficult to do; we forget. And Ike is always listening, waiting to pick out *go* in our speech.

He naps. But he still listens for *go*. One Sunday afternoon he awoke with a start. He stared. Yes, Dave and I had just finished a discussion about going. Ike had been put on alert. From that point on, he stayed wide awake, by Dave's side or mine. Ike was not to be denied because of inattention on his own part.

Go, standing alone in a conversation — Ike hears it. *Go*, a syllable, a part of another word — Ike hears it. In fore*go*, car*go*, a*go* — he hears it.

Once we thought we had a solution. We'd use a synonym of *go*. The first one we picked was *journey*. It worked.

For a time or two. And then the word *journey* was the same as *go*.

Communication is knowing, too, about the tenses that are a part of human speech. At least tenses of important verbs like *go*. The meaning of *gone* is as clear to Ike as the meaning of *go*.

Communication is knowing the meaning of a few foreign words. A couple of times Brian asked Ike, "*¿Tu quieres ir?*" Somehow Ike received the Spanish message. Thereafter, "*¿Tu quieres ir?*" brought the same response from Ike as "Do you want to go?" All four feet off the floor at the same time — a half-flip into the air.

Communication is obeying commands issued via the intercom. The voice at the other end may sound a little different, but it is still a human voice. It is one of his people speaking to Ike. It is yet another phase of communication between his people and Ike.

Communication is the Poodle sound — *Uh-huh*. A sound that with its variations covers many situations. When Ike lies down to rest or nap he takes a deep breath and says *Uh-huh*.

When he's being rubbed or patted, it's *Uh-huh-h-h-h*, up and down inflection.

Uh-huh — an answer to his people's speech. In a conversation he says *Uh-huh*, in a high tone. Or maybe in a low tone that's almost a groan — *Uh-huh-huh-huh*. Sometimes we answer Ike with an "Uh-huh" of our own.

Uh-huh from Ike. "Uh-huh" from us. Back and forth. Communication between Poodle and people.

Communication is comprehension. If we make a noise that

resembles a knock at the door and it turns on Ike's guests-are-here excitement, we can say, "I did it." Excitement dies. He understands because of the key to communication — awareness ... constant listening to and watching his people.

IKE UNDERSTANDS ... how much does he understand?

He understands the woods *goody* and the eating pleasures made possible by the goody jar — Ike's equivalent to a little boy's cookie jar. The very first dog treats were explained to Puppy Ike — "Goody, goody — a treat for Ike. Here's a *goody*." Thus a treat became a goody instead of its commercial name.

The goody jar sits in a prominent place in the kitchen. It's never empty, and it holds the goodies that reward, tempt, and appease a Poodle.

Our usual words are "Ike, do you want a goody?" but one time I asked "Is Ike eligible for a reward?" He ran straight to the goody jar, nosed it, then looked at me and barked.

Ike understands. . . .

One evening Dave said to me, "I'm in the mood to take a w-a-l-k." Ike turned to Dave and froze momentarily in a stare. Then he ran to Dave, to me, back and forth a few more times. He went to the front door and barked loudly.

Ike understands....

He was in the back seat of the car. Instead of the customary "Do you want up here, Ike?" I said in a low even voice — "You may come to the front seat." I used no gestures, a deliberate lack of inflection. Only the words. Ike leaped into the front seat.

Ike understands....

We had some people in. Ike had begged for and succeeded in getting bites of potato chips from one of the guests. Later, he came to me, expectantly, asking for a chip. I said, "Barbara is the one who's feeding you. Go back to her." He returned to Barbara, rose up on his hind feet, and touched her arm with a paw.

Ike understands....

More than a little about his people. One night Ike, with rubber ball in his mouth, came to Dave's chair. *How about a game of ball?* "I'm sorry, fella," Dave said, "I'm too tired to play." Ike — without any apparent malice — looked Dave squarely in the face, then turned and walked a foot or so away, dropped his ball, lay down beside it and took a nap.

Another evening Dave was expecting a call. He told me, "As soon as my call comes through, I'll take you for a cup of coffee." About ten minutes later the phone rang. Ike got up and stretched. With his mouth opened wide he yawned — his tongue extended all the way except for a little furl at the tip. Once the call was completed, Ike whined and shifted into his *go* excitement.

Ike understands....

At breakfast one morning we heard a noise that sounded like a BB gun. A short time later Ike wanted out. I said to Dave, "Maybe we'd better check the noise first."

"You're right," Dave answered. "If it was a BB gun Ike might get hurt." Dave walked to the door and opened it. Ike stood back, although he usually bolts out the instant the door is ajar. Dave stepped outside; still Ike waited.

"All clear. It's okay," said Dave.

Now Ike went outdoors.

Ike understands....

How much does he understand? About directions?

Ike and I returned home together in the car. Normally he enters the house with me, but this time as I opened the car door I told him, "You'd better go into the yard for a while." He climbed down and trotted to the back gate.

Knowing directions helps a Poodle keep track of his rubber ball, especially a ball that has the bad habit of getting lost. Once during a ball game with Brian, Ike's ball landed in the magazine box. Ike tried to track it. His nose was to the carpet as he sniffed, stepping on first one ear then the other. He was having trouble picking up the scent.

Brian said, "Ike, it's in the magazine box." Ike went to the box and stood there barking until Brian came to him and got the ball.

Because Ike understands, we can send him to one particular room to look for his ball. "Your ball is in the kitchen." Or "Your ball is in the den." "Go get it." And he does. If the ball rolls down the hall, maybe into one of the bedrooms, we can direct him— "Down the hall, Ike—on farther—keep going—into Brian's room."

Ike understands....

How much does he understand? About left and right?

In the car we can say, "Look to the left, Ike." And he does.

We can say, "Look to the right, Ike," and he does.

He understands because he found the key...constant study of his people and the habits of his people.

AND HE PATTERNS HIS COMMUNICATION after that of his people.

We greet each other after an absence; we greet Ike. He adopted the same habit. He barks *Hello.*

A constant study...constant because situations change. When we moved to Texas we bought a second car, which eliminated the daily practice of picking up Dave each day at the office. Ike took note of this new pattern. Each day when Dave came home I was seldom standing right at the door to meet him. On the other hand, Ike was always there to bark *Hello* even before Dave's hand touched the doorknob. Shortly after coming in, Dave would find me. Ike observed this.

Ike saw the need for a new topic of conversation between master and Poodle. Ike began a new pattern, one that's still in effect.

He tells Dave each day where I am. After he greets Dave, Ike runs back and forth to lead the way. His barks no doubt mean something like: *Come on. I'll show you where Mommer is.* He leads Dave to me. He barks again. *Here she is. Here's Mommer.*

Communication is responsibility. The responsibility of a Poodle report when we return home after Ike has been left by himself.

Activity at the front door is the subject of his reports — reliability of which was established by two incidents.

...That first time he barked at the front door after I returned home. Thinking maybe he wanted to upset routine and go out front, I told him, "No." Even after a trip to the backyard, he returned to the front door. After I opened it and showed him everything was normal, he stayed and barked. I yelled — "Ike, for heaven's sake — get away from that door!"

The next day a neighbor told me she had knocked at my door the previous afternoon while I was gone.

...Shortly after this, we all returned one evening. Again Ike stationed himself at the front door and barked. We opened the door and looked. Nothing. Ike was insistent. The next morning he resumed his report at the door. This time he wouldn't give up. Brian, with perhaps the most faith at that time in the validity of Ike's information, opened the front door to check once more. Ike jiggled all over, visibly pleased that one of his people was interested. Brian opened the mailbox. There inside it lay a circular — more than likely delivered the night before while we were away.

These two incidents convinced us of Ike's door-reporting ability.

Our confidence must have spurred him on, because afterward he took on additional duties.

If the mail has been delivered during our absence, Ike reports it to us. If the paper has been thrown, he reports it. If a parcel has been delivered, he reports it. If someone has knocked or rung the doorbell, he reports it. Even if there's no proof, we don't scoff. We may never know the details, but we're inclined to believe Ike's account of door activity.

We're believers because of the communication between Poodle and people.

Ike has the key to communication...that constant study of his people and their habits. It's a key that gives him a somewhat doubtful advantage.

For without communication, how could a Poodle dominate his family?

CHAPTER FIVE

Ike's thinking has always been mixed up.

The outlook of the canine has always been alien to him. At some point in his life—no later than the first or second week with us—he observed that his people told each other what to do. But that which was advice—an extension of communication geared to human relationships—became something else when mimicked by a black Poodle.

It became a mutation of human counsel.

It became domination.

It became ruling power.

It became Ike's own unique handling of his people.

His commands cover almost every phase of his life, and of our lives. They run the gamut from my maternal duties to his own recreation.

"Mommer, be a good mother." Be a good mother in Ike's opinion.

The scene? California. The time? Any afternoon when Brian came home from school to find me gone. It wasn't that Brian objected. He didn't. But Ike did. The action? When I came home, Ike's anger peaked. He would yelp and lunge at me the instant I opened the door. He clawed and jumped for several minutes, while eluding both Brian's and my efforts to grasp and still him.

It was a preposterous scene.

Brian tried penning up Ike in the utility room as I drove up; he tried holding Ike tightly in his arms. Tactics like this didn't erase the Poodle fury. They only delayed it. It was a fury that had to run its course, one that didn't subside until Ike punished me sufficiently for my erring ways. There was only one solution: I was to be home to greet Brian.

To be gone was the mark of a terrible mother....

Where did Ike get that queer idea? We didn't know. Its source was a puzzle that we never solved. We had no explanation. Just a label: an Ike idea. It had to be left like that.

Even though it was strengthening Ike's ruling power, I found myself actually letting a Poodle quirk be a deciding factor in my plans. I cut appointments and visits short to return home ahead of Brian. On occasion I even made an extra trip home. I often delayed running errands until after Brian arrived. This was all right with Ike. He didn't disapprove of my leaving once Brian was home.

Question: Does a dog owner dare tell the truth? "Sorry—I can't stay. I must get home. My Poodle wants me there." Answer: No. Excuses are better.

Now, in Texas, Ike still feels the same way, but he rarely has the chance to reprimand me for being absent from home when my son comes in from school. I go after Brian, and Ike goes with me.

However, Ike still has maternal governing authority. Now he tells me when it is time to pick up Brian.

From about 3:00 P.M. until departure time—half past three—Ike is vigilant. Poised. Ready. If I make the slightest move, he moves, too. *Let's leave.* His motions are jerky. Every Poodle muscle is tense. He waits for my words—"It's time to go get Brian."

Once the words are spoken, they release a gyrating whirl of black fur.

Ike has ways to tell me that it's almost time. He gets into the chair with me so that he can look me in the eye. Or with his nose he pushes a book. Or he slaps at a lamp, a newspaper, an ashtray, a figurine—anything within reach of his paw. Eventually he barks. Barking is a last resort. It leaves no doubt. *Mommer, will you please look at the clock and go get Brian?*

About 3:20 P.M. one day I was in the bedroom drying my hair.

Alerted, Ike stood in the door looking at me. Ears cocked. Tail high, the pom quivering slightly. When I made no move, he barked. He ran to me, jumped on me and barked right in my face for ignoring his reminder.

We should always go after Brian at the usual time. When we don't, when Brian because of school activities remains past the regular time, Ike is upset. He frets. He fumes. He barks. He issues *It's time* orders.

At times like this I wish Ike could understand even more than he does. Then I could explain things like school activities to him: "Ike, today is Monday. This afternoon Brian will have a debate meeting after school. We won't pick him up until five o'clock instead of the usual time." Then Ike would understand. He wouldn't think I was neglecting my motherly duties. He wouldn't get angry.

"INSPECTION TIME." Front and center. Ike dons his mental white gloves and goes on a tour of the house. As he progresses, he reports — vociferously. And we're given very little time to alter any deplorable condition he might find.

Put that vacuum cleaner away.

Close that door. Sometimes, due to the inefficiency of his people, Ike has to close a cabinet door himself. He pushes it shut with his nose and looks at us with disdain.

That purse shouldn't be there. You should know better.

That broom. You're not using it. Put it in the pantry.

Hang up those clothes.

One puppy inspection tour brought to light one terrible situation in Brian's room. Brian's oversize purely-for-fun worn-out straw hat was resting on top of the wastebasket. If there was anything that didn't belong in or on a wastebasket, it was Brian's straw hat. On the closet shelf where Ike had seen it many times — that's where it belonged. Nothing I did or said changed Ike's opinion. He wouldn't leave the spot. With dedication he continued to bark as though he had but one solitary duty to perform — the rescuing of Brian's hat. Finally, I picked up that straw hat and slammed it down on the closet shelf. Brian could dispose of it in secret later.

The hat was at last in the proper place. This pleased Ike. He stopped barking and walked off, perhaps feeling the weight of family responsibility he carried on his puppy shoulders.

In California he was particularly concerned about the neatness of his own room — maybe because of its small size and yet its dual purpose of serving as dog bedroom and utility room. Ike was resigned to laundry clutter...the soaps, bleaches, softeners, and accessories; but there were other things he did not want left out. For instance, food staples and cleaning equipment. These things were to be put away in the pantry in the utility room. If they were scattered about, it disturbed Ike and often instigated a complete inspection tour, starting with his own room.

In rainy weather, when not in a clown mood, Ike wouldn't tolerate wet towels in his room. He demanded that they be put on a rack inside the pantry; he barked until his wishes were carried out.

There were still other articles he felt shouldn't be in his bedroom.

After a basketball game one night Brian hung his gym clothes in the utility room, intending to put them in the soiled-clothes hamper the next morning. He had to reckon with Ike. Ike *demanded.* He demanded that Brian's clothes be removed. Should a fellow have to go to bed with dirty, wet, smelly gym clothes hanging over his head?

Ike was not always so unreasonable about clothes hanging in his California room. There I often hung articles of clothing still slightly damp from the dryer to finish drying. Ike accepted this as part of clothes washing and drying routine. He allowed it.

To a point.

When *he* felt the clothes had been hanging long enough he would tell me to put them away. He wasn't being unfair; he had given the clothes — and more important, had given *me* — ample time.

I suppose Ike will always pull inspection on us because he still has great enthusiasm for finding wrongs in the house. Not long ago I was running the usual race with the clock, readying the house for a party that night; I had a mental list of things yet undone. When Ike started his something-is-wrong barking in the kitchen, I was giving the guest bathroom a pre-party going over. I put down the sponge and the cleanser, washed and dried my hands, and went to the kitchen. There Ike stood looking at the countertop. Did I know that the big party coffee maker was there on the countertop? Who took it off the pantry shelf? What did it mean? There was no smell of coffee. It was just sitting there. *Aren't you glad I found it?*

An inspection tour can disclose almost anything. Even a suitcase on the bed. Dave had returned from a business trip and hadn't yet completed unpacking. Ike barked and tried to push the open suitcase with his nose. *Put this away!*

Dave answered, "I'll put it away, Ike, when I finish unpacking."

Ike barked. *Put it away. Now!* He tried again to shove the suitcase. If it had been lighter, Ike would have pushed it to the floor.

Still Dave didn't do as Ike wanted. To emphasize his point Ike stretched, over the suitcase, took up a handkerchief and tossed it into the air.

Inspection time. Where's the den clock? It was being repaired. Ike would walk to the hearth, stand directly under the spot where the clock should hang. A look at the empty wall, and a bark. How could a Poodle and his people keep a routine without each timepiece in its right position?

Inspection time. It's cold! How does a Poodle tell his family to get a fire blazing in the fireplace? He noses the firescreen, looks at his people, and barks. If it's a wish of moderate intensity he asks once and then gives up if there's not an immediate people response. If he is especially desirous of a fire he repeats his request emphatically. It becomes an order. *I want a fire.*

FOOD AND WATER... Ike considers the demands of his tummy legitimate reasons to issue orders.

Give me food. My water bowl is empty. Feed me now — right now.

Give me a bite of that meat on the countertop. Before barking his request, he may try his own powers first. Forepaws on the edge of the cabinet. Eyes in line with the meat. He gazes with concentration. He tries to will the food to come to him. Watching him, you can almost hear eerie music, can almost see the meat lift up and slowly float through the air, drawn to the mouth of Wizard Ike.

This is Ike's *levitation nose* at work. And he practices his power quite often. He must have immense faith that someday he'll be able to levitate a chunk of meat.

As is inevitable, his levitation nose doesn't prove successful, and he must revert to people-bossing. Ike desires, so Ike demands...a bite of meat.

Ike barks his demand usually to me when I'm preparing dinner. And on occasion this meets the same failure as his levitation nose — but all is not lost yet. Three plans are used to get a bite of the dinner meat. Levitation nose, bossing, and the third and last is Dave...a plan I don't believe I've ever seen fail. The drawback is that Ike has to wait until Dave comes home from the office.

When Plan No. 3 is engaged, Dave is met at the door and greeted briefly by an anxious Ike. If Brian is home Ike tries to get Dave to bypass the father-son greeting. *Hurry, Popper.* Ike leads him to the kitchen. *Here's Mommer. In the kitchen where she's supposed to be.*

Dave and I kiss. Ike tries to bypass this greeting, too. *Look. Look at the meat.* He barks, standing at the cabinet or at the stove if the dinner meat is already cooking. He shows Dave. *I want a bite of that.*

The tiny bite Dave gives him appeases Boss Ike.

I want my meat tidbits. Another meat demand. This time *after* dinner. Each evening when we finish our meal, Boss Ike orders us to go to the kitchen so that we may serve him his tidbits. Of course, he would eat a large portion, but a small bite from each of us is all the custom requires. It's actually a token sharing of the dinner.

But token meat or not Ike demands what he considers his. When we are slow about leaving the dinner table, Ike becomes the dictator. He stares at us and barks. If we don't move, his patience dwindles...until suddenly all patience is gone. That thrusts him into the highest degree of tidbit-time exasperation. He walks the floor and claws at the first item that catches his eye.

One evening our conversation delayed Ike's meat tidbits for an unusually long time. He went to the coffee table and with a disciplinary nose shoved each magazine, each accessory.

Ike demands food, whether it be bites of the human kind, or his own canine food. He always has.

When he was a tiny puppy we started him on the usual four meals a day. It wasn't long before Puppy Ike took over. He barked for his food, and when finished he barked for his bowl to be taken up. It seemed — with four meals a day — to be a constant series of demands.

Food. Dish down. Dish up. Water. More food. Dish down. Dish up.

He grew, and we cut his meals to three a day. Then, two a day. When he was eight or nine months old we began to feed him only once a day, in the evening.

A new schedule...Ike seemed pleased with it. He asked for his one meal a day in the evening. We gave it to him when he asked for it. It worked well for a few months, until Ike was about a year old. And then the new theory evolved: If Ike could demand and get food at the time his people had scheduled, *why couldn't he demand and get food anytime Ike wanted it? On an Ike schedule?*

...Demand feeding. Ike demand feeding.

That was the new feeding schedule. That was the way it would be from then on.

No longer was Ike's mealtime decisions the duty of his people.

Ike's demand schedule...most of the time it's two meals a day. But Boss Ike makes the final decision. Sometimes he throws in a variation, and I'm not convinced that it isn't more to show his authority than to follow the dictates of his stomach.

We, Ike's people, have often said, "We hope we never have to put Ike on a reducing diet." Just as it was almost impossible to restrain him from getting more than the one meal a day, it would be equally as difficult to limit his food intake.

Give me food. He still barks for his food about half the time. The other half he bangs his food dish. With his nose he flips up the metal bowl, which clangs on the floor. Or he pushes the bowl against the wall and then paws it as if it were a punching bag.

Once we start to put food into the bowl, Ike leaves his eating station. He goes across the room, at least . . . maybe into the next room. He knows when the serving is completed—even if he's in the next room—and he then returns to his bowl to eat.

It's just the opposite while he waits for his water bowl to be filled and returned. He doesn't leave, but sits down and waits. Where? On his eating mat, in the exact spot allotted to his water bowl.

Give me food. Once, when Ike was ravenous, he started to eat with great, choking gulps. Suddenly he stopped. Not to get his breath, but to bark at me. He took another bite. Again he looked up at me. He swallowed then barked again.

I didn't know what Ike wanted me to do. In this case Ike prevented a failure of my understanding. He showed me. He scooped up another bite, went to the pantry door and barked. This time he hadn't swallowed, and food spilled out his mouth.

Now I guessed what he wanted.

"More food?"

Bark. Yes.

"You're sure?"

Bark.

I put more food in his bowl. He resumed eating—still gulping. But now the amount of food was better proportioned to his appetite.

Give me a goody. Goodies aren't always rewards. Boss Ike may go to the goody jar and bark to demand a goody just because Boss Ike wants one.

I want a frankfurter. Ike called me to the kitchen. He was in front of the portable broiler oven, barking. We had cooked frankfurters in the oven an hour or so earlier.

I said, "Ike, you had a bite of our hot dogs at lunch."

He answered . . . a look at me, a look at the oven, another bark. I got a small piece of frankfurter from the refrigerator and gave it to him. No more demanding.

Another time he barked me to the kitchen, but not for a frankfurter. In fact, not for food at all. Even though he led me to his eating station, I saw that there was food already in his bowl. I turned to leave. He barked me back.

Each time I tried to leave, he barked. What did he want?

I was failing again to understand a Poodle order. I stood still a moment, thinking, figuring. By standing there I inadvertently did what he was trying to tell me to do. He began to eat.

He wanted me to stand by his side while he ate.

I almost failed another time . . . when Ike called me to the pantry door. He didn't want the food I put in his bowl. There was nothing out of place in the pantry. I said, "Forget it, Ike," and went into the den. I called him to me.

He came, but a moment later he returned to the pantry door and barked me in there again.

I went. I called him away again. He returned; he called me. I actually began to feel stupid not being able to understand a dumb animal's request. There had to be something very fascinating that Ike had discovered in the pantry...or maybe *smelled* there....

Of course. I finally remembered. About a week earlier I had put a package of chew bars on a shelf. I placed them high, thinking their presence would remain unknown to Ike. Then I forgot.

"Is it a chew bar you want?" I asked. "Is that it?"

A series of happy, happy barks. The welcomed pleasure of a chew bar evidently helped him overlook my lack of intelligence.

WE, IKE'S PEOPLE, should be honored to serve him.

Boss Ike rules. His people follow.

You, I choose you.

He makes the call for a special service. He decides which of his people is to serve him. *I choose you.* No one but the selected one will do.

...Ike was sitting in the kitchen by the back door. His look said *I want out.* Brian opened the door for him. Ike stood up but wouldn't go out. Brian shut the door. Ike's look became more urgent. Dave went over and opened the door. Ike stood still.

Ike eyed me. *I choose you, Mommer.* When I opened the door he trotted out to banish the urgent look.

...Ike's people were eating cookies in the kitchen. Dave asked Ike, "Do you want a cookie?" A superfluous question really. Ike had never turned down a cookie.

Dave had made the offer, but I followed through. A little maneuver that made a difference to Ike. I broke off a bite of cookie and offered it to him. He took it into his mouth slowly, reluctantly.

He didn't chew it.

He moved over to Dave and dropped the piece of cookie at Dave's feet and glanced up. *I choose you.* Dave picked up the bite and presented it to Boss Ike.

Things once again in balance. The proper person following through. Eagerly Ike now ate that bite of cookie and several more because the sharing was executed correctly by his people.

...Ike banged his food bowl. When I went to the pantry to get his food Ike ran to Dave and barked.

I asked, "Do you want Dave to get your food?"

Several barks. *Yes, I choose Popper.*

Dave had been tapped for service, and he answered the call.

Just before he began to eat, Ike gave a soft little bark. We took it as a bit of praise from Boss Ike. This time, at least, his people carried out his wishes very commendably.

... Ike always chooses Dave for nail care. If I get his nail clippers or file from the shelf, Ike always runs to Dave. Dave asks, "Do you want me to do your nails?"

Barks convey the answer. *Yes, I choose you.*

... There is a difference when Ike chooses Brian. Although Dave and I may be selected to perform only *one* Poodle service — when Brian is chosen, it is for multiple causes.

Ike often chooses Brian for breakfast service each morning. Ike issues the first command to Brian, and the response is seldom fast. During the interim Ike carefully avoids looking toward Dave or me — the unchosen. He usually has to bark at Brian again, has to repeat his original order for breakfast. Brian can prolong service and get away with it; Dave and I receive no such Poodle tolerance.

Once Boss Ike has been fed, Brian may receive an order for water service. Or, with ball in mouth Ike may issue this order: *Brian, I choose you to play with me.*

Brian elaborately tells Ike, "I don't have time — I'll be late for school." Ike insists. And Brian, as always, finds the time.

Ike may demand that Brian let him out. Brian protests — shortage of time again. But Brian complies. Ike knows that for him Brian can stretch time.

Why not? It's a part of people servitude. It's a duty to perform for Boss Ike.

"I'M A MESS — DO SOMETHING ABOUT ME." One day Ike summoned me to the utility area. I remembered that time in the pantry when he asked for a chew bar, for once again I couldn't figure out what Ike wanted. I employed the method of elimination. Ear medicine? No. An old toy that had been put on the shelf? No. I showed him numerous things. No. It was none of those he desired. He'd look at each article I presented to him and turn his head back to the shelf again.

Finally, I had shown him everything except grooming tools. I picked up a brush and said sharply, "I guess this is what you want."

Bark. Bark. Bark. Joyful barks. *Yes. Yes. Yes.* He jumped upon me trying to reach the brush.

I didn't have time...I had other things to do...things that were left undone while I, like Brian, stretched time. As I brushed that Poodle coat, I couldn't help but think it was absurd for *Ike* to be the one to decide he needed to be brushed.

None of his commands are ever ridiculous to Ike. His theory is that the services he wants should hold the same amount of pleasure for his people as for Ike. If they don't, it's due to misguided ideas of his people, not the fault of the commands.

Ike's commands seldom are forced. They emanate in a natural way. There was another brushing session, this time *my* decision. I had everything ready. "Time for a brushing, Ike. Come on." He started, then hesitated. He turned around, ran to his bowl and ate one bite. Then he ran to me and barked.

Mommer, you wait! I want to eat first. Back to his bowl. One bite. A look then to see if I were waiting. To see if I were obeying. He finished eating and came to me. Barks. *Brush me. I'm ready now.*

A brushing...a full grooming job...Ike commands. After Dave and I became Ike groomers, one night we clipped only Boss Ike's feet. With the most tedious part out of the way I could finish him alone the next day.

A logical grooming plan it seemed to us. But not to Ike. When we put the equipment away on the shelf, he was there observing. He began to bark. A look of disgust is a look Ike can manage, and he had that look now.

I really am a mess.

He stood on his rear feet, pawed at the air, tried to reach the clipper box. He barked—a sassy bark.

The Lady never waited until the next day. She didn't put away the clippers after only his feet were done. She had respect for the appearance of her friends. She knew how to groom Poodles. And he had tried so hard to show us how to groom him the way The Lady had. One thing was now clear. He would never have an efficacious grooming plan until he gave his people additional education.

IKE WAS IN THE BEDROOM WITH ME. I was barefoot—no particular reason...the carpet just felt good under my feet.

Barks. *Where are your shoes?* I thought I might go barefoot all day. Barks. *Where are your shoes?* I was alone, except for Ike. Who would care?

Ike would.

He had no shoes; therefore he went barefoot. I had shoes; I should wear them.

And my shoes were in the closet, where Ike was now. Barking, he was. And clawing at my shoes on the closet floor. *Put these on.* He looked at me.

And shoes not on human feet should be in the closet, allowing perhaps for a good reason otherwise—like canvas shoes that have been washed and are still drying. However, when they are dry, it is a signal for Boss Ike.

Late one afternoon from the patio I brought Dave's canvas shoes to the kitchen. I didn't take them to the closet because I stopped to begin dinner preparations. When Dave came home Ike didn't greet him. His boss duties took precedence.

Ike stayed in the kitchen by the shoes and barked loudly, calling Dave. Ike even withheld his after-an-absence enthusiasm when Dave came into the room. The shoes came first; they were dry and ready to be put away, and nothing would be normal until this task was done. *Put them away!*

Dave took his shoes to the closet. Then Ike greeted him properly.

If I forget shoes that are drying on the patio, Boss Ike does not. One night at bedtime Dave went out with Ike. When Ike was at the door, ready to come in, he suddenly saw my terry house shoes on a yard chair. He ran to the chair and pushed my shoes with his nose. He barked at Dave. *You're not leaving Mommer's shoes out here, are you?*

No, Dave wasn't—not after Boss Ike had found them. The two of them came inside to me, Dave carrying the shoes, Ike wiggling with pride.

Pride because of the importance of his boss duties? Pride because he had maneuvered Dave so well? Pride because he had done something for me?

IT'S INEVITABLE.

There comes a time when it seems natural to receive certain orders from a Poodle. It seems natural to *obey* certain ones.

Ike's will dominates.

I want that chair. And he usually gets it.

He has a favorite. The wing chair. But it may be another that he demands if his mood calls for it.

I want that chair. It's a natural request. Bossing is a tiring activity. Why shouldn't a weary overseer select a comfortable chair in which to take a nap? The only problem is when someone is sitting in it.

How does Boss Ike remove that human? There are different approaches. One is the no-nonsense approach. Ike merely stands in front of the encroacher and barks. *I want your chair.*

There is another more spirited approach. Ike circles the room several times at high speed then narrows his circle to ring the desired chair. He leaps and lands — a panting, black heap — in the occupant's lap. If this doesn't defeat the human, Ike slithers behind and roots and shoves to clear out his chair.

And there is the human-guilt approach. Ike walks slowly, stiltedly, back and forth in front of the chosen chair, his eyes on the person sitting in it. He may climb up into a substitute chair, but he isn't defeated. This approach is one slow to develop. From time to time he gets down and walks back to the chosen chair. He stares at the human and manages to look extremely sad and rejected. *Look at me. I'm so tired. It would help to be in that chair.* He is helpful. He shows the person another chair in which to sit. He points it out with barks and looks in the correct direction. With cooperation, the chair Ike wants is vacated.

I want that chair.

More often than not, Ike's choice is his favorite wing chair. Once Ike wins, once the chair is all his, he climbs up into it, turns round and round, and snuggles down into a black ball. Before long he snakes out, flips over on his back into a semicircle of upside-down Poodle — all four legs straight up. This is such a favorite position I think it is why he prefers the wingback, which is an exact fit to enclose the curve of Ike.

Sleep comes, sound sleep, dream sleep. Ike is an energetic
dreamer... he barks. He makes eating sounds and movements with
his mouth. He runs with fast, twitching motions of his feet. He wags
his tail.

Once after getting his chair sleep wouldn't come. Ike couldn't
settle down. Over and over he made his preparatory circles. He told

Dave his trouble. Ike looked at the bright light of the lamp by the
chair. Then he looked at Dave. At the lamp, at Dave. *Turn it off.*
Dave did. Ike put his head down and went to sleep.

I want that chair. Once it is Ike's, he growls at a possible tres-
passer.

IKE, ETHNARCH OF THE LUSK household, speaks. *Listen to me,*
he says.

He speaks to Dave: *Get moving this morning. Get to work. It's
late. Routine is dragging. Quit drinking coffee.*

It's the same every morning. Ike has to get his family moving.
People can be so difficult. They must be prodded.

And not just in the morning, but all day long. Day in. Day out.

One night Ike went to the den door and barked. Dave opened the door and watched Ike run all the way through the garage, and out into the drive where the car was still parked.

Listen to me. You left the car out. Dave did listen to Ike's barks. A bit sheepishly Dave drove the car into the garage for the night.

Listen to me. Open those drapes. Ike wants to look out the window. At once. A series of quick, demanding barks. *Open those drapes.* If we're too slow Ike dashes to the middle of the drapes and shoves his head through.

Listen to me. Constant prodding. Constant maneuvering of his people.

One day Ike wanted out. He scratched the back door, barked, and sat there. *I* didn't think he really needed out. I called him to me and made him get up on the couch by my side. He glared at me. His eyes were about six inches from mine. He growled, softly at first. The growl intensified. His eyes still on me, he then barked. A single, loud, command bark issued with a puff of hot dog breath on my face.

I got up and opened the back door. He proved to me he really did need out.

Listen to me. As emphatic a command as *I want out* is his *I want in.* In or out, he issues the orders. We obey.

"GUESTS, YOU LISTEN TO ME, TOO." Not only does Ike censure female guests for leaving their purses out, but *all* guests are subjected to his ruling powers.

Once when we had weekend guests Ike called me into the guest room. From the middle of the room he was taking a visual survey. His eyes went from the unmade beds to the open closet doors to the open suitcases.

Have you ever seen such a mess? Boss Ike doesn't allow any leeway on the part of guests. No laxity of neatness just because a person is visiting.

Guests, you listen to me. When in Ike's house, guests are ruled and handled the same as his own people are. After getting completely acquainted, if Boss Ike decrees it, a guest may be commanded to feed him, to give him water, to play with him, to let him out and in. Boss Ike decides the Ike service with which to honor a guest.

Guests are subjected to Boss Ike's rule. So are neighbors. Neighbors? Yes. Ike doesn't like boundaries on his authority. He proved this point that day when he was on his chain, watching a California neighbor build a fence. The midday sun was warm, and the neighbor pulled off his jacket and hung it on a fence post.

That he shouldn't have done.

Ike told him he shouldn't have done it—told him with steady barking, barking that brought me to the yard. I sized up the situation just before the neighbor asked me, "Why is Ike barking at me?"

I felt a little foolish when I answered. "It isn't *you*. It's your jacket—hanging on the post. That's what he's looking at."

"You mean he wants me to move it?"

"Probably."

The neighbor stood still a moment. I suppose he was trying to decide if he dared give in to the whims of a yapping black Poodle. The fact that he owned two Poodles I'm sure swayed his decision in Ike's favor. He reached out, took his jacket, folded it, and placed it on the ground. "There, goofy," the neighbor called to Ike. "Is that better?" It was.

From the windows our Texas neighbors are bossed by Ike when they walk around in their own yards. He fusses at them when they go to and from their cars. Either they aren't supposed to do these things or else in Ike's opinion they are doing them incorrectly.

THERE ARE THE PEOPLE WORDS "Take me for a walk." A command. An order.

In the utility area Ike barks. On his hind feet he stretches toward his shelf. A throaty growl. A bark. At this point he could be asking for any of several things, but when he runs to the front door, barks, and hurries back to the shelf, the meaning is clear.

It's his way of saying our words "Take me for a walk." It's an order.

"PLAY WITH ME." Ike is in the middle of the den. He calls us to him. His barks are singles, with pauses, each one a bit more determined than the last. *Now. Play with me now.*

Once he has banished our nolition, Boss Ike decides which kind of play to pursue.

Run play? That's especially for Dave and Ike. Dave chases Ike to one end of the room, then Ike chases Dave to the opposite end. Dave laughs. Ike barks and playfully nips at Dave's heels. Another turn. Both at the same time. To watch them is to be reminded of choreography.

Hand play? There are two kinds of hand play. The first is simply a mock battle between people hands and Poodle mouth. The second is a little more complex. We lie on the floor on our backs and run a hand underneath the body to the opposite side—where Ike lies waiting. When the hand appears, he nips at it, fights at it.

House bone play? "I'm going to get your bone," we say, but we don't really get it. This is the signal for Ike to get his bone and come growling to us. *Don't you get it.* He tempts us by lying very close as he chews. A hand reaches out. He growls. *Don't you get my bone.* He drops it into a lap. *Don't get it again.*

Ball play? If his ball is in plain sight Ike picks it up and brings it to us, barking with the ball in his mouth. His muffled *Play ball with me* command barks sound like yaps from inside a burlap sack.

Play ball with me. If his ball isn't in plain sight Boss Ike issues another command: *Find my ball.*

"Get your ball, Ike," we tell him. I have never understood why he always knows where his house bone is but seldom the whereabouts of his ball.

Barks. *(You find it for me.)*

He may follow our instructions and retrieve his ball. Or if we are hunting it for him, Ike is the spectator with a worried look. *Where, oh, where is my ball?*

The delay of a hunt for the ball adds zest to the game.

Play with me. Like so many of his habits, demand play began when Boss Ike was a puppy...when he first started to study his people...when he first discovered he could demand and receive... when he understood that the *second* time could be repetitive.

CHAPTER SIX

IKE DIDN'T DEMAND ANY KIND of play the first few days he lived with us.

Neither did he demand playtime with Dave the first few nights. There had to be a beginning. He had to be shown what my husband was willing to do for the sake of Ike entertainment.

There was a first evening when Dave stopped reading, folded his newspaper, and fulfilled a sudden urge to play with Puppy Ike.

That was it.

That was the one time it took.

The second night of game time with Dave was preset now. And the third. And the fourth. And all the times through the years.

Ike has a right that shall be forever denied Brian and me—and any other human. Ike can come up from behind and hit the newspaper Dave is reading without provoking his master.

That open newspaper is the cue. Game time with Dave. No ordinary playtime is it. This night game time is special. This is the same ritual of play that Puppy Ike and willing Dave began a long time ago. No variations.

It starts with a canine body thrust against the newspaper. Ball in mouth. Ike stands with forepaws on Dave's arm. Expectation. Suspense. Pent-up energy. Shaking head and playful growls. No usual ball game, but a combination of tugging, and throwing, and retrieving.

Who stops the game? Dave or Ike? Either one. It doesn't matter. There are never any recriminations against the one who tires first.

When it's over, Ike lies down on the newspaper Dave has put on the floor by his chair. (I suspect it is for Ike's pleasure that Dave places the paper on the floor.) To lie on Dave's newspaper is part of the pattern.

That's the way it was done that very first time. It was a natural thing to do because Ike was already familiar with newspapers.

And maybe he developed a lifetime respect for newspapers because of that early affinity. Memories, so many memories associated with newspapers...puddling on them...shredding them for fun. The faint smell of ink...the familiar rustling sound...the feel of it under his body, his feet, his head.

But there is something softer than a newspaper to lie on.

Pillows. Big pillows. Little pillows. Square pillows. Round pillows. Oblong pillows. Any shape—as long as they are *soft*.

Again there had to be a first time. When was it? When was the initial pillow introduction? It was the first time Puppy Ike and I went by ourselves in the car and my driving precluded holding him as I had done while Dave drove. Missing the comfort and security of my lap, Ike began to tremble and whine. I pulled over to the curb and from the back seat got a car pillow, put it close by me, and put Ike atop it. No more trembling, no more whining...until the next car trip, when he wouldn't settle down until he was nestled down on the pillow again.

The car pillow was small—about eight inches square. It had been used for a head rest until Ike took it over. As soon as he was too large to recline on it, stretched out full length, he was too energetic anyway to lie down during a thrilling car trip.

But use of the pillow wasn't forsaken. When he no longer lay on it, he sat on it. He would turn round and round and back up to it, then lower his rear to the pillow like a hen settling down on her nest.

With all the use it was bound to happen. The pillow wore out. Ike hunted for substitutes—a sack of groceries, a parcel, anything on which to sit.

Puppy Ike found house pillows, too. He found them on the love-seat, in chairs, on the beds. Almost everywhere were pillows. Except in his own bed. One day before he chewed the sides off his bed he asked for a pillow of his own.

He took a small throw pillow from Brian's bed and put it in his own bed. When I removed it Ike growled and tugged at it.

He got a pillow. I made one for him with a cover of washable, sturdy terry cloth. When I put it in his bed he knew immediately it was his. He knew it was another personal possession, an item

belonging only to Ike. This pillow, because it was Ike's, was there-fore unlike all the other pillows throughout the house. Family pil-lows were those others. And family pillows—the big ones, the small ones, the fat ones, the thin ones that Ike liked to lie against or on top of, one or a whole stack—were to be shared. Ike's didn't have to be shared. It was his to do with as he chose.

His socks, his rags were personal possessions, too. A small child often finds great delight in playing with discards—an old pan, a spoon, an empty can. Puppy Ike's treasured discards were old socks and rags. He considered them equal to his other toys, with one ex-ception. Mouse. No toy—no plaything—was equal to Mouse.

An old sock with a knot tied in the middle...we gave the first one to our puppy to add a little variety to his play. With zest he took to it; he clamped down on the knot with a good firm grip and tugged and growled, and tugged and growled. When the game was over, he took the sock to his room.

"Go get your sock, Ike." And a sock joined the rank of playthings to be brought forward when Ike was asked to do so.

With two males in the family, I had no trouble gathering up a substantial stack of Ike socks. Ike saw me put them on a shelf in the hall closet. He understood. He remembered.

He still remembered days later. That first sock ultimately became limp, shredded masses of heel and toe held together by a narrow strip of sole. I was forced to throw it away.

Ike posted himself by the hall closet and barked. He wanted a new sock. I gave him one. That was the *second* sock. The pattern had been established by the first one. Or perhaps it went back... to a time even before the first sock... back to that second day—the open house... back to the gift of cloth, the pad for his bed....

Ike may think each new sock is a gift from us.

And each rag, although gifts of rags aren't as frequent as socks. We limit rag gifts, a practice Ike would like to see abolished. When he sees a rag in use, he begs for it. He knows the difference between a rag and good fabric. How, I don't know. Is it the look, the smell, the human uses? If I'm polishing furniture with a piece of old cloth Ike will sneak up behind me and make a grab for the cloth.

When he sees a small rag torn from a larger one he begs.

Any kind of rag. Ike saw Dave tear the canvas cover off a yard chair so I'd have a pattern to make a new cover. Ike jumped up and grabbed the canvas, which after the ripping was now just a rag.

A rag or a sock can often be found in Ike's bed.

But then his bed has always been a multipurpose thing to Ike. Other than a cache for stolen items, it is also a storage unit for toys, an eating spot.

Eat in bed? Why?

Because there was a first time.

When he was a puppy he found that a bite of people food was often too big for one bite in a puppy mouth. And a bite that was a little too large could be messy, with crumbs—perhaps greasy ones —dropping to the floor.

Dave hit upon a procedure—of doubtful merit, even had it remained temporary as Dave intended. He gave Puppy Ike a bite of food, told him "Take it to your bed," and showed him what he meant one time.

One time. And then a lifetime of crumbs in his bed. A lifetime of surveying bites....

Unless halted by his people, a tidbit is an automatic run-to-your-bed order. Once there he either chews while standing with only his forepaws in his bed, or he keeps all four feet on the floor while he leans forward to get his head over his bed. Can't let crumbs fall to the floor...must keep them in the bed.

And those bites of people food are to be hand-fed. They should never be put in his bowl. Once Dave put some cookie pieces in Ike's food bowl. Indignantly Ike picked up a bite, took it to his bed and ate it. Then back to his bowl for another bite — to his bed again to eat it. Back and forth, until the bowl was empty. Each trip spawned a new look of annoyance aimed at Dave.

It was fitting that Ike should be displeased with Dave, for Dave of all people should have remembered about hand-fed bites and eating in bed. He had started the whole thing in the first place.

Dave had a knack for bed training. And eating in bed wasn't the first training phase. The first was that day when Dave was dog-sitting, and as puppies are apt to do, Ike forgot he was housebroken.

And as masters are apt to do, Dave forgot about patience. Not wanting to take the time to escort Ike to the yard in true training procedure, Dave plucked up Ike — "You go to your bed. Shame on Ike!" — and tossed the repentant pup into his bed.

Ike has always responded to Dave's commands — more readily than to Brian's or mine. This was perhaps the first evidence of that obedience. The next time Ike had the urge to relieve himself, he tried to please Dave. He puddled in his bed.

There had been a first time. It was difficult, very difficult, to break the habit his Popper had begun. We'd take him outdoors; he'd perform as expected. But he gallantly performed as he thought was expected indoors, too, even though we scolded him. For weeks there were damp spots on his bed pad. Gradually they appeared less frequently.

Then at last we *thought* the idea of puddling in his bed was eliminated.

The emphasis shifted from Ike's bed to the more acceptable backyard, where another application was initiated. As he matured, relieving himself became a dawdling, perusal-of-the-yard time. Impatiently we'd say "Hurry! Ike, hurry!"

Hurry. Good word. Meant perform on cue. It still does. There are hurry trees, hurry bushes, and even stunted, hurry flowers. In fact, the backyard is one big hurry room.

But the yard isn't restricted to hurrying.

Where else but there could take place the experience of a first yard bone?

A first real bone. A strange but enticing object of puppy curiosity. A thing of undetermined value until instinct nudged Puppy Ike. Instinct told him to gnaw it, chew on it. He pushed and rolled the bone around until the fur on his face, ears, and paws was plastered down with a mixture of grease and saliva. Instinct turned a clumsy start into a professional finish.

The second yard bone was fresh out of the freezer, thawing on the countertop. Ike found it and called me to the kitchen. Barking, he ran back and forth, from the cabinet to the back door.

Finding a thawing yard bone wasn't unusual. Seldom is there anything on the countertop that escapes him. Once, while making sandwiches I put a small piece of lunch meat to one side — to the left. Ike was standing, upright, at my elbow. I said, "That's Ike's," and gave him the bite.

The second time I pushed some bits of food to the left side Ike barked steadily.

That's Ike's. Puppy memory.

That first time...just one time!

Puppy memory that wouldn't let go.

Puppy memory that locked in patterns from the first time. *"Toro!"* A lifetime game. *"Toro!"* Brian called to Ike that first time and held his shirt like a toreador's cape.

Puppy Ike responded. Sure, he'd play with Brian. With his head low Ike charged the shirt. Just as he got close, Brian lifted the shirt, and Ike's momentum carried him a few feet farther. Ike turned, surveyed the arena. Brian jiggled the cape. *Olé*. The black bull charged again. *Olé*. *Olé*. The agile toreador was ready....

Puppy memory. And a first time from the car one day. Ike saw a cat sunning itself on a brick planter in a corner yard. Ike jumped to the window, howling. I believe the old Siamese cat who tormented Ike in his own yard was responsible for his excessive animosity toward cats.

The next time we drove down that street Ike tensed up. As we neared that same corner house, he went to the appropriate window. There was the cat again.

From then on, Ike was always watchful when we drew near the cat corner. If the cat were there, Ike went wild. If the cat were not there, Ike still acknowledged the corner by growling softly.

There was another special California corner. The newsman corner. On our way to Dave's office each afternoon, at *that* corner Ike would look for the newsman on the opposite side of the street. After we picked up Dave and started back, Ike got set to see his friend. When the traffic light was in Ike's favor and we had to stop, the newsman ran over to the car and patted a wriggling, happy Ike. I wonder how many sales the man lost by giving his time to a Poodle. When we had a green light, or when we were too late, or too early, and missed seeing Ike's little newsman friend, Ike was visibly disappointed. He whined and gazed at the corner.

WHEN WE MOVED FROM CALIFORNIA to Texas we drove through by car, but Ike came by jet. It was his first airplane trip.

There hasn't been a second one — only facsimiles.

One night we were watching television, the volume turned fairly loud. Ike was lying close to the set. On the screen a jet landed — there was a loud thump when wheels touched runway. Ike sat up.

Reverse thrust, and the roar of the engines increased. Ike cocked his head to one side, then to the other. He listened. Somewhere... sometime... it was as though he had to dig into memories... as though he had to match this sound with a corresponding one in the past. Hidden somewhere in Poodle memory was that first time.

AFTER THE MOVE IKE HAD TO REPLACE the California corners with new ones in Dallas. No cat corner, no newsman corner, but he found a German Shepherd corner, a Beagle yard, and a mixed-breed block.

And there's a crossing guard corner about halfway between home and Brian's school. Each time we drive past, the friendly guard waves to us. In return, Ike barks a *Hello.*

New corners in Dallas... other new habits.

The first time Ike went with me to the drive-in window of our new bank, he was pleasantly surprised. He had been to drive-in windows before — but never to one like this.

When the banking business was finished, the cashier reached out and gave Ike a dog biscuit.

Ike's reaction the *second* time couldn't possibly have been different than what it was. We drove up to the bank. Ike pushed his head out the driver's window. He was taut with anticipation. Then came the dog biscuit. All according to pattern — but a pattern that wasn't to last.

A few months later the bank deleted one of its customer services — the canine treats. Ike was shocked. He couldn't believe it. He barked. Perhaps the girl had forgotten. He'd remind her. She smiled sweetly at Ike and said, "I'm sorry." Being sorry wasn't as good as a dog biscuit.

Ike barked. She looked helpless. He barked again. He barked as we drove away. He barked as long as he could see the bank from the rear window.

The bank moved to a new location — new building, new drive-in windows. But it was still our bank, and Ike knew it. He still expected his dog biscuit, still barked his dissatisfaction when that treat was not forthcoming.

A bank cashier asked me one day, "Does your dog remember when we gave out dog biscuits?"

"Yes," I answered.

"You wouldn't think he'd remember, would you?"

I would think that. Yes. Especially when Ike carried his bank grudge to other businesses — to the dry cleaners, to the drugstores, to the food-to-go restaurants, to any drive-in window. It's always the same. He stands, rear feet on the back seat, front feet on the back of the front seat, head out the driver's window. He waits — until any necessary business is taken care of.

Then the instant business is over Ike barks. He barks as the car pulls away. *I used to get a dog biscuit!*

For Ike, I suppose there will always be new first times. He's always ready to grab onto a new habit and never let go.

I was sewing in the guest room. Ike started to jump upon the bed where part of my sewing was spread out.

"No!" I yelled in time.

He waited while I cleared off an Ike-size space. I pointed to it and said, "Okay. Right there." Up he came. He didn't move from his designated spot until he needed a drink of water.

When he returned, still licking his mouth, he stood at the guest bed and barked once.

I said, "Okay." Up he jumped.

Unless there are unusual circumstances, Ike barks for permission to get on the guest bed if there is anything on it. His Mommer told him to do this, and he is remembering her instructions.

There must be a first time for Ike. And then the second time informs us we have a new habit with which to contend.

A short time ago I gave Ike the opportunity for a habit. Early one morning before I opened the back door to let him out, I happened to see his house bone lying by his bed. I said, "I'm going to get your bone." If I felt playful so early in the day, he wasn't about to let my mood go to waste. He grabbed his bone and climbed into his bed with it.

I feigned a pass or two at him. He growled but kept the bone conveniently turned to me.

I let him out. The first time for early morning house bone play was over.

Was there a second time? And a third? And on and on? Yes. Often now, before he visits the hurry tree, he gets his house bone, runs to his bed and growls at me. *Don't you want to get it?*

How does Ike decide what will be retained and become a habit and what will be rejected and forgotten? We don't know. Therefore, we often ask: "Will this be one of those first times?" Now we try to think twice before we do anything for him, to him, or with him —something we didn't know when he was a tiny puppy.

We try to think twice. Sometimes we forget.

Sometimes we're lucky.

One Saturday morning, when we were in no hurry to get up, I got Ike and put him in bed with Dave and me. There was a second time—an early, early morning bark. About 5:00 A.M. *Come get me.* We were lucky because it was stopped with the second time.

"Will this be another first?" Ike was with us in the car, and he needed a hurry stop. We parked at a branch library, where at the edge of the grounds Ike found an ideal hurry bush. "What if he demands a stop here each time we pass?" we asked.

Retained or rejected. Which would it be?

Living with Ike, it's impossible not to wonder often if another first is being created.

If *we* don't know how Ikus P.Q.R.S. Aroonus selects those retained firsts, *he* knows.

And once they're added to his collection of crazy patterns, he'll remember them, if need be from one year to the next.

Ike remembers. . . .

CHAPTER SEVEN

IKE REMEMBERS HOLIDAYS.

From one year to the next he remembers.

Remembers good holidays. Remembers bad ones (all of the Fourths of July). Remembers a brief holiday like Halloween, or a group of days with a climax like Christmas. And a very personal holiday like a black Poodle's birthday. Holidays are made to be remembered. Remembered they are.

They are in the Poodle memory, ready for recall, ready to assist in the identification each year of the current holidays . . . the special Ike days.

HALLOWEEN — A PLEASING Poodle memory. All orange and black and pungent is Halloween. Made for excited children and for excited Poodles.

For Ike, Halloween began as a time of adulation from spooks and goblins whose eerie purposes melted at the sight of our baby Poodle.

"What a darling puppy." "Oh, it's precious." "What's its name?" "May I please pet it?" "It's so cute." Why is it that children always use the neuter gender when referring to puppies and kittens?

Ike had come to us on Thursday. His unofficial open house had been the next day, on Friday. Then the following Sunday was Halloween. Perhaps he considered Halloween an extension of that open house; perhaps he thought he was still on display. Perhaps he was.

Again and again the doorbell sounded. "Trick or treat!" "Trick or treat!" People. Little, friendly, loving, Poodle-petting people.

A canine trick or treater, too. Abernathy came to our door; he barked; Ike barked back; Aby received a treat; so did Ike.

The biggest treat of all to Ike was Halloween itself—the excitement of the doorbell announcing so many children.

He remembered, and the next year he was ready. When again the California autumn came in its gentle way, when the peach and apricot trees shed their leaves for Ike to chase in the backyard, when the ocean sent a breeze that felt slightly damper and cooler to him—it was time again for Halloween.

He watched. I got the big wooden bowl, filled it with candy, and placed it by the front door. Ike reached back in Poodle memory... somewhere there was another time...when food was put by the front door in that same bowl.

And then the first group of trick-or-treaters came. A finger pressed the doorbell button.

Doorbell. Food in a bowl by the door. Excitement. Of course. The children!

Halloween!

But no more of that passive, tiny-puppy celebrating. Not for this, his second Halloween.

He tried to leave with that first group of children. I guess he wanted to make the rounds of doorbell-ringing and treat-seeking. (Did he remember that Aby did that the year before?) By the front door I pulled up a chair, and when the next children came, I commanded Ike to climb into it and sit. Thereafter, when the doorbell rang, Ike barked an answer and leaped into the chair. He liked this arrangement; he didn't try to leave again.

Twitching and wiggling happily, he greeted the masked and unmasked. From his new vantage point in the chair he could sniff the treats in the bowl. He could be petted by the monsters, the princesses, the princes, the apes, the spacemen, the skeletons, and the other spooks—all with hands that smelled of dirt, of apples, of popcorn, of chocolate, of chewing gum.

Finally the doorbell was quiet.

The last hobgoblin had petted Ike, had been treated, and was gone.

The big wooden bowl had been filled three times and was now nearly empty again. It was late...we were tired...Ike was tired, but as if he heard some kind of silent doorbell, he slowly climbed into the chair once more and gave the bowl a gentle push with his nose. He whined softly.

It was a reluctant farewell to his second Halloween. A farewell to a holiday that was now a Poodle memory.

In Dallas, autumn began with more force. This Ike discovered shortly before his third Halloween. In Texas it was nothing as subtle as a slight change in an ocean breeze. The outdoor world drastically turned to dry brown. The air became crisp...almost cold.

Ike nosed the lawn that was now dead. He listened to the paper-crackling sound when the wind fingered the dried clusters of mimosa pods. He lifted his ears when a pod would burst open and he investigated the seeds that fell to the ground. As the other trees defoliated, Ike chased their leaves.

He had found one thing that was the same in California and Texas. Leaves. Falling leaves.

Autumn had come to Texas. And it brought Ike's third Halloween.

Once again, at dusk on Halloween, I got out the big wooden bowl and filled it. I took it to the foyer and Ike barked and nipped at my heels.

Where's my chair? Where's my chair? It's Halloween!

This year instead of a chair, I pushed a hassock to the honored spot by the front door. For most of the evening Ikus P.Q.R.S. Aroonus sat upon the hassock, and when there'd be a lull he'd bark and look at the bowl of candy. There was no doubt; he preferred a steady stream of little people.

The adulation of the first two Halloweens was still his.

The children couldn't ignore the friendly black Poodle head that suddenly jutted out when the door was opened. They recovered quickly from the startling sight of Poodle eyes on the level with theirs. They patted Ike's head.

They talked lovingly to him. They praised him, and he acted as if he had just been elected Poodle-of-the-Year. He accepted it all as his due on Halloween.

Several times, between groups of trick-or-treaters, we left the door ajar so Ike could listen to the sounds of Halloween...to the laughter and squeals of children making their rounds through the neighborhood...to the noisemakers...to the tooting of horns...to the distant barking of dogs.

THE SOUNDS OF HOLIDAYS in the Poodle memory...there is a sharp contrast to the pleasant fun sounds of Halloween.

It is the Fourth of July with its harsh, reverberating noises.

Ike heard the popping of firecrackers that first Independence Day. But he was not upset. He was not afraid. He listened, then nonchalantly went about his business of playing, eating, sleeping, and ruling his people. He didn't know he was supposed to be afraid.

He didn't know that some dogs have to be tranquilized and then still spend the Fourth of July quivering in the bathtub or under a bed.

He didn't know he was supposed to react to firecrackers.

But by the second year he began to know. Somehow by then instinct told him he was to be afraid.

Fourth of July fear was a progressive emotion. By his third Independence Day, the crack of the first firecracker early in the morning caused him to yelp and run to me for protection. He wasn't without at least a feeble retaliation. He barked, but it was definitely unconvincing.

When Brian got up, Ike barked a steady conversation to him. *Firecrackers, Brian. It's that day again. Bang. Isn't it terrible? They're all around. In the yards. In the alley. Listen. They're so loud.*

And louder they got. Much louder. By night it sounded as if all of North Dallas were under attack.

With the exception of the aggravating noise and the lingering aroma of explosives, it was a nice summer evening. We were eating homemade freezer ice cream on the patio, under the mimosa that had zippered its leaves for the night.

Ike loves homemade ice cream. Any other night he would have been there waiting for his share. But not tonight. He was indoors.

Now and then we'd see him peeking out the den window. We begged him to come out. He ignored our coaxing. We took him some ice cream. He refused to eat it.

At bedtime, Dave had to pick up and carry a struggling Ike to the middle of the yard, had to retrieve him several times from the back door and return him to the yard. "Hurry, Ike. It's bedtime. You have to hurry."

Hurry? In the midst of a battlefield? Hurry? With bombs bursting all around?

At least it was bedtime.

Another bad holiday was over. Gratefully, Ike relegated another disquieting Fourth to Poodle memory.

NONE OF THE BOISTEROUSNESS of Independence Day. Just a song. A song to celebrate a special day...a personal holiday. "Happy birthday."

A song to lock in a Poodle memory.

A little boy who has his first birthday has a cake with one candle. Some little boy Poodles have birthday cakes, too. Ike did. It was a chunk of angel food, and struck in the very middle was a single blue candle. (It was Brian's decision to use the blue-for-boy candle.) Dave, Brian, and I sat at the kitchen table for the birthday song and cake-cutting ceremony. Ike stood on his hind feet, his front feet in my lap, stretching his head forward, trying to reach his cake and the burning candle. His nose wiggled as he sniffed the cake, and his breath made the little flame flicker.

"Happy birthday." That meant a big piece of cake, all his own, instead of his usual token bite of dessert. "Happy birthday." It meant gifts—a new rag, a chew bar, and a rubber bone that lasted two days.

"Happy birthday." Those words were put into Poodle memory that first birthday and have since meant a special Ike day. A very special day. People loving. An extra share of attention. Gifts... from near and far.

For his third birthday, he received a parcel post package from California people friends. We told him, "This is Ike's."

He barked, and danced, and pawed at the package as he tried to help open it. An appreciated gift it was—a giant chew bar.

Our gift to him was a new house bone, all gift-wrapped and tied with a perky bow to be dog-wilted with damp breath and wet tongue. A new bone... not one to replace the old house bone, but an addition to it. Now there were two bones to step on. Two bones to stub toes on. Two bones for Ike to hide in our shoes. Two bones for him to put where he so desired.

"Happy third birthday, Ike," we said to him.

"Happy birthday," said a card that came in the mail . . . addressed to "Ikus Aroonus Lusk."

Gifts. A card. And for this third birthday a cake baked by me especially for Ike. No makeshift chunk of angel food taken from the freezer at the last minute like that first birthday. No complete lack of cake like the second birthday. But on the third birthday a special Ike cake. On it three lighted candles waited for the puff to extinguish them and seal the wish at the same time. But how do you tell a Poodle to make a wish? Brian was concerned that tradition would be slighted, so he blew out the candles, and I think probably made a wish for Ike, too.

"Happy birthday." A birthday song. The next year, when he would be four years old, there would be a birthday song again. And a cake, and gifts. And love.

A BIRTHDAY IS GOOD. It is gladness . . . and happiness. But there is a much bigger holiday, one that doesn't unfold and climax in a single day. This one lasts for days, even weeks. By Ike's people it is called *Christmas.*

His first Christmas quickly became for Puppy Ike a composite of the good things of all holidays, the good of all the special days rolled into one season. People, family, friends, neighbors. Loving atmosphere. Good food—unusual food. And gifts, but more than for birthdays. Gifts for everyone.

The little fuzzy bear cub that was Ikus P.Q.R.S. Aroonus noted in detail the many rituals of a Lusk Christmas that first year. One such ritual held particular interest. When he saw it he stood perfectly still for a moment, his tail straight up. Immobility was brief, because curiosity moved him to the big *tree* that Dave and Brian brought into the living room.

Yes, it was a *tree.*

A real, green, full-of-outdoor-smells tree. But it wasn't outdoors where trees usually are. This one was inside the house. And then he watched his people begin to do such strange things to it. Strings of colored lights first, and that took a long time . . . with the adjusting, the talking, the rearranging. Then at last the lights were right.

That wasn't all the attention the tree was to get. There were still remaining all the full boxes, the cartons with the garage smell. Ike climbed up and looked into one or two of them. He saw extracted from the depths of the boxes shiny, glittering things—some of them like balls that surely wouldn't be much fun to play with. Ike observed; we slipped hooks into the decorations and hung them on the tree branches. When we'd permit it, he smelled the ornaments as we handled them.

About halfway through the tree-trimming project we were ready for a break; so was Ike. We had refreshments — coffee, milk, and Christmas pound cake. Food is always a good holiday ritual in Ike's opinion, if enthusiasm can be a measuring device.

When we were ready to continue, Ike was also ready. He stayed with us until the last ornament was in place on its appropriate branch... each felt and sequined decoration, each jewel-encrusted styrofoam ball, each glass ball, each metal bird, each gold angel, each elf. The tree was gently slid into the corner by Dave's chair. Only one more tree ritual remained. Ike smelled the white felt tree skirt that I took from its tissue paper nest; he stood at my feet while I placed it around the base of the tree.

Then Dave turned on the tree lights.

The human members of the family felt the joy that a newly decorated Christmas tree brings. The canine member climbed up into Dave's chair, stood with his hind feet in the seat, his forepaws on the arm nearest the tree. One branch extended almost to the chair. Ike sniffed that branch. Did he decide at that moment, or was it later?

We looked at the tree. "Perfect," Dave said. "Beautiful," I said. "Fine," Brian said. We thought the tree was completed. It wasn't.

The next day there was one more decoration on the branch by Dave's chair.

It was Ike's contribution to the tree.

It was his beloved Mouse, Ike's most treasured possession. There, nesting on the broad branch, Mouse stayed throughout the Christmas season. More than once Ike climbed up into the chair, gently touched his nose to Mouse, then with a pleased look got down and moved away.

The next Christmas there was no Mouse. But there was a tree.

A tree. A tree in the living room. That unlocked Poodle memory. *It's Christmastime!* All the days of good things to be climaxed by the big Day.

...All the good things. First, the tree trimming.

And then the other decorating... including a new, small stocking hanging with the other three. This one, red with a white cuff, bearing three sequined felt appliqués — a ball, a bone, and a fireplug.

The big gold basket with poinsettias on it was put on a table. The first Christmas card that went into it was Ike's. It was from his father, and mentioned sincere wishes for the best doggone Christmas ever. It was signed, "Pepe."

Gifts were under the Christmas tree. New ones were added daily. Packages of all sizes, all shapes, with angels, gold and silver medallions, bells, tags, ribbons, and wiggly bows. All to tempt a curious Poodle. Ike succumbed slightly to temptation; a couple of bows resembled wilted flowers. Just two wrinkled bows...nothing else. Ike was a good boy.

He was enjoying Christmastime.

...Ike smelled Christmas. He smelled the pre-Day cooking aromas...the spices, nuts, fruit, the candy, the bread. He smelled the tree, the pine cones, the bayberry candles.

...Ike heard Christmas. He heard the music from the stereo... heard the songs that were dominated by chimes and bells and church voices. He listed to the tape of the band performance at school—especially to the resounding "Hallelujah Chorus" finale ...listened as though he could pick out the sound of Brian's clarinet.

...Ike heard Christmas when the carolers stopped at our house and sang "Silent Night."

...Ike heard Christmas each time the front door was opened and the string of bells jingled.

Yes, Ike was enjoying his second Christmas. There seemed to be no doubt of that. He knew the rituals of the season—so well, in fact, that he reminded his people of them.

For instance, the tree lights were to be turned on at dusk. If we forgot, Ike stood at the tree and barked until the tree was illuminated.

His Poodle memory told him the Day would come. Until then, he waited as the days of the season passed...some with the warmth of Eastern spring and others with Southern California's brand of snow—fog. That opaque, damp, soft fog that settled over everything, muffling the familiar sounds. It even erased Aby's house. One pre-Day morning while Ike yelped and strained against his leash, the old Siamese cat walked through the backyard and disappeared almost magically into the marshmallow fog.

The card basket filled. Many cards included Ike's name, but one more came addressed specifically to him. It was from The Lady... French motif...with pictures of two elegant Poodles.

When the card came, elegant was the last thing in the world that Ike was.

His shagginess and drooping topknot proved it was time to go see The Lady. The 22nd of December was the date of his standing appointment. It couldn't have worked out better. He would look handsome for Christmas.

And he did. Unusually handsome.

The Lady added a special Christmas touch. Ike came home wearing around his neck a wide red velvet ribbon trimmed with a green net bow.

A new dimension of Christmas. Something pretty for Ike to wear. That night we tried to remove his Christmas collar. Ike pulled away. He growled. *No. Don't take it off. The Lady put it on me.* All right. We left the collar alone.

By Christmas Day Ike still looked handsome. The collar didn't. But to Ike the dirty, twisted thing around his neck was beautiful. It was the spirit of Christmas, a gift of love. A gift from The Lady.

There were other gifts, the ones under the tree. And on the Day, there was the ritual of gift-opening. An exciting event for Ike. Underneath all the paper and ribbon there were the presents of Poodle toys and chew bars. It was fun to help open the people gifts. Such interesting smells of leathers, metals, perfumes, paper, and new cloth (that would someday be lovely rags).

Guests came to have Christmas dinner with us. This pleased Ike. He met them at the door and barked, probably telling them about the goings-on, the gifts, the funny looking Christmas meat in the oven.

Of that Christmas meat, Ike got his share — a big serving of turkey drumstick. Then, while the people lingered over pumpkin pie and coffee, Ike put his levitation nose to work. He stood on his hind feet at the kitchen counter, trying with all his might to levitate that holiday bird—to levitate it to the mouth of Ikus P.Q.R.S. Aroonus.

I'd like to have what's left of that turkey.

Especially dedicated to his Christmas levitation, Ike barked and barked, his eyes fixed on the turkey, that lopsided turkey that was still fat on one side and nothing but exposed carcass on the other. When we'd go into the kitchen Ike would acknowledge our presence with an almost imperceptible tilt of his head, but he never moved his eyes away from the turkey.

Another Christmas was almost over when that holiday bird was deboned and wrapped for refrigerator and freezer. Then it became just meat and no longer the impressive bird that had reposed on the kitchen countertop.

But there would be other turkeys. There would be other Christmases, also, to add to Poodle memory. Next year there would be his third Christmas.

Ike's third Christmas...the holiday with the big problem.

CHAPTER EIGHT

AT THE BEGINNING OF IKE'S third Christmas season his actions were normal. And then suddenly the big problem emerged.

When alone, Ike became Mister Trouble.

In the Dallas house there was no way to pen him up in the kitchen. Although there was a door into the foyer, there was none between the kitchen and den, and architecturally it wasn't feasible to put one. When we moved in we decided to trust Ike with his freedom. After all, he was a mature dog. It would work out. The mischief of the months that followed was negligible when compared to that of his third Christmas.

Alone.

Alone with all the Christmas paraphernalia.

Mister Trouble.

Mister Trouble...alone with the Christmas tree....

That first time, it seemed so incredible we refused to accuse Ike and dismissed the thought completely. We were to blame—"...it happened when we added water to the tree holder."

But the second time the blame had to go to the proper source. We *knew* we hadn't added water to the tree holder. The spot on the carpeting was larger this time. Also, the felt tree skirt was wet. Drops of moisture still clung to a tree branch and to an ornament hanging on it.

Our Christmas pine had become a hurry tree.

"Ike! Did you do this?"

R-r-r-r.

"Why did you do it?"

R-r-r-r.

We dragged him to the spot, shoved his nose up against the wet branch, and spanked him.

R-r-r-r. Upper lip peeled back over his teeth.

The spanking didn't solve the problem. Neither did a commercial spray designed to deter canine urges. When left alone in the house, Mister Trouble continued to lift his leg at the base of the tree — not every time, but when he decided he wanted to do it.

My poor tree skirt. I couldn't forget the long hours I spent making it, sewing on the hundreds of sequins and beads. Some of the sequins had already rusted. It shouldn't be washed — yet here I was, spot-washing the tree skirt each time Ike violated my handwork. In the beginning, I thought each time was the last, but finally to preserve the skirt I took it up when we'd leave.

But we couldn't take up the carpeting. We were grateful it was showing no ill effects from the spot-sudsing and drying.

Washing couldn't restore the low-hanging tree ornaments. A few that escaped rusting were broken when they hit the floor — knocked there either as Ike brushed by them, or else by a recalcitrant paw. These were old, plain ornaments. We had already moved all the hand-decorated ones to high positions in the tree. Every time we had to cut off a damaged lower branch, our tree was more and more like a woman who lifts her hemline with changing fashion.

Ike also tried to open some of the gifts already under the tree. He shredded gift wrapping and scattered it about the room.

"Did Ike do this?"

R-r-r-r-r.

"Shame on Ike."

R-r-r-r-r.

Shame on Ike. Shame on Mister Trouble.

It hadn't always been *Mister*. When he was little, the name was Puppy Trouble.

Puppy Trouble. Trouble of various shapes and form. When he set his mind to it, Ike could leave a trail of puppy havoc from the front door to the back, and into the yard.

Trouble could be holes dug in the backyard. That is, it was trouble when we didn't want holes dug in the backyard. And we preferred smooth, unbroken green lawn to brown patches. Ike didn't. He thought the ground under his chain was his.

"No. No, Ike." We'd point to the hole and spank him.

Sooner or later there'd be a new hole, and beside it a flattish mound of soft, newly turned California earth. He was a powerful puppy digger. Three or four feet away from the hole, the dichondra would be sprinkled with the rich, dark brown dirt.

A new hole meant a hole to be filled and tamped.

Then we had a double problem. Each single hole became two holes.

Ike had a dirt-moving assistant. Aby.

We'd look out the window and see both Poodles hunched up, digging as if it were a contest. I don't know which dog won, but the people lost.

We lost, and lost, and lost.

We lost each time there was a damp spot in Ike's bed because we thought we had won. We thought we had erased entirely the idea of bed puddling. Good for us. It was a partial win, however, because he chose to retain bed puddling as an occasional means of revenge.

We lost when I had to launder all his bedding.

And then there was less to launder. One day there ceased to be a perfect balance between puppy mischief and pillow preservation. His personal pillow, the one I had made for him, was demolished. By his own mouth and claws, he was without wicker bed first and now his pillow, too.

What prompted him to attack his pillow?

Was it the same kind of urge that induced him when he was about eight months old to chew up his dear Mouse?

Was it a sudden flash of hate for Mouse? Did he decide Mouse had been *different* long enough and should now be treated the same as other worldly possessions, even to the point of deserving Poodle wrath?

No toy since Mouse's demise has been shown the honor that for a time was Mouse's. If a plaything lasts, it's because of special material or construction and not due to preferential treatment by Ike.

Mouse was destroyed. Mouse was gone. We didn't punish Ike, for in some way it seemed his right to decide Mouse's fate.

But punishment was not ordinarily withheld.

It wasn't that day, quite sometime later, when Ike ransacked the bottom desk drawer. While I was out of the room he found the drawer open, and Mister Trouble began to work. He smeared the labels on the file folders, pulled out receipts and records, took out the entire current bill file — scattered its contents about the room. He mangled a year's supply of monthly insurance notices — the do-not-fold-spindle-or-mutilate-computer-card kind.

"Did you do this, Ike?"

R-r-r-r-r.

Could he deny it? Perhaps not with the evidence — the drawer contents — spilled out on the floor, but he might have explained it. . . .

We were in the middle of moving preparations.

His people were upset. That was the best reason of all for Ike to be upset.

And when a Poodle is upset, he's apt to be destructive. Shame on Ike. The desk drawer was just the beginning. "Shame on Ike." We said it many times during the moving interim.

People coming and going . . . realtors . . . prospective buyers . . . relatives of prospective buyers . . . friends of prospective buyers . . . Ike resented being hooked to his chain while strangers poked through his house. When they'd *look* at the backyard, Ike would almost choke himself trying to reach them. When they'd leave, he would have to inspect every inch of the house. Even the closets weren't private with this new kind of caller.

And Dave was away — in Dallas — except for weekends. It all meant something. Ike didn't understand what.

A baffling situation. So for the first time in months, Ike chewed off the hair on the bottom of his ears.

Still a baffling situation. Ike tried something else. While penned up in the utility room he found a new tension release. The washing machine cord. He chewed it, and chewed it, and chewed it. There were little short pieces, one to two inches long, all over the room.

When I telephoned for a washer service call and explained what kind of repair was needed and why, the girl on the other end breathlessly asked, "What happened to your Poodle?"

"He's fine."

"He didn't electrocute himself?"

"No," I answered. "He unplugged the cord first."

Ike was not through chewing. Not by a long shot.

Even with The Lady, that very last clip date, he was naughty. "Tell them, Ike," The Lady said. "Tell your people what you did."

His tail went between his legs. His head lowered. He had chewed up his leash.

After the move many things were different, but at the beginning of Dallas life, Ike was still on the same old chewing spree.

Chewing mischief.

A lamp cord gnawed in two while we were away, but—naturally —it was unplugged first. Dave patched it with electrical tape. The next time we returned home the same lamp cord was chewed in two again.

"Did you do this?"

R-r-r-r-r.

We spanked him.

R-r-r-r-r.

It happened again and again. *R-r-r-r-r.* When confronted, he always growled. He had found an act that displeased us, and for some reason that ostensibly gave him pleasure. Once when Dave spanked him for chewing the lamp cord, Ike growled as usual and then abandoned restraint in a blast of wrath. He bit Dave's spanking hand and then spent the remainder of the day in his bed.

Finally Ike left the lamp cord alone. Either he tired of the same old rubbery taste or our response weakened to such a degree (What's one more patch on a battle-scarred lamp cord?) it was no longer serving Ike's purpose.

Besides, the freedom of the house when he was alone afforded Mister Trouble a choice—a veritable smorgasbord of mischief possibilities. One time the choice was a leather handbag I had left on a chair. All his life he had been telling me to put purses away. Now he showed me. He disciplined me by damaging one.

Another choice was to claw a door. Deep, ugly scratches put there with angry paws.

Another was to gnaw on magazines.

Even when he was *good*, we'd return home to find footstools overturned, sofa pillows on the floor, end table appointments pushed precariously near the edge.

When he was bad, he knew it.

Once after punishment he stayed in his bed for a very long time. He did bark for permission finally to leave his bed. "Okay," I called. "You may come in here." He ran to me, jumped up into my lap, and lovingly snuggled up against me like a contrite child.

The months in Dallas passed, and for a brief time Ike's misconduct leveled off. No new distressing habits. His actions stayed in the *good* range — confined to minor offenses like rearranging lamps and other articles on the tables. We felt he had adjusted to freedom when left alone, and that he preferred this to the old way of being penned up.

We were wrong.

Christmas was the catalyst.

We had a problem — one that didn't go away when Christmas was over and the tree removed. Now Mister Trouble found other substitutes for the indoor hurry tree.

He used the back of Dave's chair.

It was a manifestation of stubbornness. It was a Poodle's unwillingness to relinquish an old way.

It was resentment. It was the fault of his people, too, for failing to see the reason for that resentment.

We tried every possibility but the correct one.

One thing we tried was a cessation of spanking. We felt that perhaps this would solve the problem. One day as I sponged a hurry spot on the chair slipcover, I wanted desperately to punish Ike, but I held off. I was willing to try the new approach. No spanking it would be.

And it seemed to work. No new spots in a whole week. We lavished loving attention on Ike. He seemed to thrive on it. We had at last solved the problem.

Only superficially.

The next time our obdurate Poodle lifted his leg on the chair I wondered why I had always thought I loved dogs.

I had cleaned up too many indoor hurrying spots. I had tried to outguess a strong-willed Poodle too many times.

This time was too much. I sat down on the floor by the chair. My eyes filled with tears, and there was no holding them back. I cried. I cried loudly. I cried for all the times I hadn't cried. The more I heard myself the more I cried. Ike slipped up to me and started to lick the tears streaming down my cheeks. I didn't push him back. I just cried more tears for him to lick off.

After quite a time he moved back and barked several times. *Please stop, Mommer.* I kept crying.

He came back to me, and I put my arm around him.

There had to be an answer. There was. We had tried other things that hadn't worked. Why not try a repetition? The only thing we hadn't tried—a door, so we could pen up Ike in the kitchen when we left him. In spite of architectural design, Dave made a portable door of lightweight paneling—a half door, similar at least in size to Ike's California room door.

Ike's door, we labeled this one.

Ike's door was the answer.

He liked it from the first.

It must have given him a secure feeling immediately . . . but then it was logical. Hadn't he been penned up like that all of his life in California?

Ike's door is less than three feet high. He can jump three feet from a standstill. Without a running start he could clear his door any time he wanted to.

If he wanted to.

Basically the door was the answer. It restored a right; it ended an all-out hurry revolt. It cleared up a big misunderstanding. But a door—or anything else could never completely eliminate Ike's occasional grudges against his people. Not when he lives as close to us as he does. Shame on Ike...nearly all his grudges are because he can't go everywhere with us.

When Ike believes he should have been allowed to go with us, he shows his perturbation in varying degrees, to be exact—three.

The first is mild irritation. His *frustration jar* takes care of it. Didn't get to go? *They'd better take me next time,* and he walks over to a low shelf by the breakfast table and with his nose shoves a little pottery sugar jar. Sometimes we find the jar balanced on the edge of the shelf; its lid may be propped up on the rim, like a hat at rakish angle on a head. (It's Ike's jar now; we donated it to the cause of Poodle temper.)

The second degree is more intense, too much so for the frustration jar. He *shows* us we should have taken him...he drags dish towels to the floor, and also the breakfast chair cushions. The rug under the breakfast table is pulled back, and he claws at the pad underneath. Anything left on the table—mail, newspaper, basket of fruit—is pushed to the floor.

The third and final degree of animosity is shown in an old, despicable way that's reminiscent of that third Christmas. Instead of the Christmas tree he lifts his leg on the dishwasher. But now that he finally has his door and is closed up in the kitchen when alone, he reserves this action for extreme cases. It has only happened a couple of times. Both incidents qualified, in Ike's opinion as extreme cases. He was left at home when it was time to pick up Brian at school. He was cheated out of two car trips.

To go in the car to school is an unalienable family right for Ike. He believes this.

Now we believe it, too. We are aware of his rights, and when we deny him we expect the consequences. If possible we try not to deny him.

We indulge him.

CHAPTER NINE

THE MOVE FROM CALIFORNIA to Texas meant details piled on top of mountains of worrisome details. One little mountain was reserved for Poodle details...shot records...travel plans...boarding arrangements in Dallas. When at last Ike was put in a kennel aboard the jet he was in a halcyon condition.

Ike calm?

Ike placidly entering into an adventure like a first flight? When a common event like the ringing of a doorbell can turn him into a whirlwind of black fur?

But the ordinary Ike didn't take that flight. Aroonus the Pampered did. Pampered and *tranquilized*. Sedated to banish trepidation.

Tranquilized to afford him the dignity his veterinarian felt he deserved. "Ike flying to Texas?" the vet asked over the phone. "My high-strung friend Ike taking a jet? Well then I'd certainly suggest tranquilizers for the flight. Bring him in—I'll check him over and give you the pills."

The vet dispensed the tranquilizers to me. To Ike he gave some last ear-scratching and body-patting. *Uh-huh*, Ike said.

For the last time Ike delivered a volley of barks to everyone in the vet's office. On his hind feet, forepaws on the counter, he talked to the vet and the receptionist as I paid the bill.

"Good-bye, Ike."

Bark.

"We'll miss you."

Bark.

A pampered Poodle was all set for his trip. The right to be tranquilized—an addendum to an already-long list of rights.

Some are Poodle birthrights: grooming, care, food, and a certain amount of love.

But other rights—the overflow of love, the humoring, the indulging, the liberality, the pampering, the babying, the favoring, the immunities granted, the gifts from house guests, the collar that's fancy even though devoid of stones—these are Aroonus rights.

Aroonus rights—a pampered Poodle's Magna Charta. There is no protesting, no struggle to win his personal rights, for they are already established. They are now rights accorded to Aroonus the Pampered without question. They are his due. They are many....

THERE ARE THE AROONUS PLACEMENT RIGHTS.

His people should not challenge his Placement Rights. If we do, no points are won; there are no favorable results. We only irritate a Poodle.

I gather up two house bones, a ball, a sock, perhaps a current toy, and rag or two. I put them in a neat stack in a half-hidden spot. *I have violated Placement Rights.* In a very short time each item is returned to its former position.

When Ike was a puppy, I had what I thought was a good idea. I donated a basket to the Poodle toy storage cause. Not only did Ike reject the idea (he would immediately empty out every toy after I filled the basket), but he finally won his point in a most personalized way. He chewed up the container.

Placement Rights become in reality clutter rights when they relate to a big rag. Until we make an irrefutable people-decision to end the life of a rag in the wastebasket, we don't fight Ike's right to put a rag where he wants.

The problem is that a rag doesn't remain *a* rag. With Ike's help it multiplies, not unlike cell division. Rip. A rag becomes two rags. Rip. One of these two rags becomes two more. Rip—rip—rip— and Ike has the right of placement for each one.

The home of ragpickers. That's the picture of our house when

Ike has a big, prolific rag. That's why a rag cannot be a permanent possession of Aroonus the Pampered.

THERE ARE BONE RIGHTS—but without reference to Ike's house and yard bones. Even an unpampered dog is given minimum bone rights.

A special, an above-normal favor is granted Aroonus when his people have a certain kind of bone—the small chop or steak bone, the chicken leg bone, the blade bone—the usual end-of-the-meal bones. Even though these are more in evidence than the veterinarian-approved big knuckle bone, we can't, of course, give one of them to Ike.

But Dave or Brian can hold it for him.

As is true with any kind of after-dinner tidbit eating, the kitchen is the setting. Male people-hands with a firm grasp on a bone make it possible for Ike to nibble off the little bits of meat that escaped human eating implements.

Never does Ike try to take the bone. He recognizes the kind he can't have for his own manipulation. When he has finished in one spot he waits for the hands to rotate the bone to a meatier position. He's always gentle—slow and methodical. Never so much as a hint of a snapping bite.

Ike will not let me hold a bone for him. If I offer one he backs off and barks for Dave or Brian to come hold it. It's strange that he refuses my assistance. If the reason isn't that he thinks bone-holding even for a gentle Poodle isn't a suitable activity for Mommer, then perhaps it's because he prefers a masculine grip.

My only alternative to fulfilling the obligation of Ike's Bone Rights is to pick the meat from the bone and hand-feed him.

IKE DOESN'T OBJECT TO BEING HAND-FED. In fact, that is one of his Eating Rights.

Hand-fed. Over a hand place mat. When he surveys a bite of food given to him and decides he should run to his bed to eat, he can be stopped. "Here, Ike—here."

We hold a cupped hand down to his level, and Aroonus walks to it, puts his muzzle over the up-turned palm, and begins to chew. There's probably in Ike's judgment no nicer crumb-catcher—not even his bed. After the bite is gone, the crumbs are there waiting to be consumed; and when the crumbs are gone the crumb-catcher turns into a head-patter, or rubber, or scratcher.

Eating Rights include for Aroonus at least a small bite (preferably more) of every good food we eat. *Good*, naturally, is defined with deference to a Poodle's palate. If the food is a soft, nonfinger-feeding type, he has the privilege of eating the bites from a fork — maybe not as expertly as people but fairly well, considering the necessity of more tongue use than that of a human gourmet.

Pampered people often have breakfast served in bed. A pampered Poodle does, too. Not his regular dog food breakfast, but his people food breakfast tidbits. Like followers of some ancient cult, one at a time we file by the animal god on his bed throne and lay our sacrifices — a bite of toast, or a bit of bacon — at his feet.

Aroonus accepts it graciously, regally, like one who has been served often and well by his people.

THE SERVICE HE ACCEPTS may be breakfast in bed...or being tucked in as a child is.

To be tucked in is his due, because Aroonus has Cover Rights. We have noticed that breakfast in bed is asked for much more often in the winter, when the right of cover is also granted.

On a cold morning he makes a perfunctory trip to the hurry tree and hastens back to the warmth of the indoors. At his bed he waits until someone lifts his blanket. Then he climbs in and settles down. When we tuck the covers around him, he sighs loudly. *Uh-huh-h-h-h.*

There he stays — during breakfast and during after-breakfast coffee — until his people's morning routine demands that he rise.

Cover Rights apply also at bedtime. Aroonus the Pampered has a *cover me* look. It's a pleading stare; there's no mistaking it. Especially on a very cold night when he is still shivering from a prebedtime visit to the hurry tree. Then his *cover me* look has a special urgency to it.

Early morning, and bedtime. Cover Rights chase away the quakes and quivers brought on by cold, make a Poodle feel loved, make him feel warm and secure in his own bed.

But Cover Rights extend beyond his own bed. . . .

"COVER ME." ON THE LOVE SEAT. *Cover me.* On the couch. *Cover me.* In a chair.

Cover me. With my afghan.

It's an Aroonus right to have an afghan of his own in the first place, in the second place to have *Ike* embroidered on it.

Is a nap more pleasant when he's covered with his own afghan? Aroonus knows the answer.

He has known it since the original right was altered.

The afghan's primary purpose wasn't for cover. When Ike was a puppy I made it for a furniture protector; it was spread out when we allowed Ike to use people seating facilities.

Puppy Ike had good afghan manners. He would halt at the front of a chair and wouldn't jump up until the afghan was in place.

Even after he matured he respected the afghan's purpose. He still did for a while after the move. And then for some reason he stopped asking for the afghan. We share in the evolution of the Afghan Right because we didn't enforce the original rule.

Now when he asks for his afghan, it's a *cover me* request. When we don't notice the *cover me* look, Ike punctuates it vocally.

One wintry afternoon I lay down on the couch and spread Ike's afghan across my legs. I dozed off. Ike's barks awakened me. He was standing with his forepaws on the couch looking first at his afghan then at me.

I lifted a corner of the afghan and said, "Okay — come on up." He jumped up, made the required circles, then lay down by my side. *Uh-huh-h-h-h.* We shared the afghan. We often do. I never get to use it alone. Ike sees to that.

I get the impression that Ike is trying to revise the Afghan Rights once again to give him sole use.

THERE ARE NO PEOPLE INFRINGEMENTS on Sweater Rights. We can share his afghan, but certainly not his sweater.

What possible use could we have for a bright orange tube that looks as if it may have been knitted for an elongated Dachshund? On Aroonus the Pampered it is very becoming. The brass buttons add just the right debonair touch.

Ike doesn't wear it often — only when it is extremely cold. It isn't that Ike doesn't want to wear it more. Once it's on, he doesn't want it taken off.

The summer day I finished knitting his sweater, Aroonus modeled it, preening like a woman with her first fur. The temperature was 100 degrees that day, but when I'd try to remove his new garment he'd pull away.

Sweater Rights yield the privilege of people-type clothing. Ike likes that. And when frost has decoupaged the yard with ice crystals I'm certain he doesn't overlook the comfort benefits of his sweater.

I'M CERTAIN BECAUSE IT would be unlikely for Aroonus the Pampered to overlook anything related to his comfort index.

Pillows are Poodle comforts, a belief Ike has had since that first pillow in the car.

No fancy throw pillows in this house. No satin, no velvet — no fragile, delicate, expensive fabrics on our pillows. They're all Poodle oriented — both material and construction. (There's a possibility we can't overlook — that of another Poodle pillow-destruction time.)

A well-groomed, noble Poodle looks magnificent perched atop a satin pillow. In a picture. On a greeting card. Or in a thought.

In reality—no. Realism asks for homespun pillows.

Especially for Aroonus and the playful side of Pillow Rights. The unrestrained enjoyment of sliding on his belly up to a stack of pillows and burrowing under them. A sudden flip of the Poodle head. An explosion of pillows. A colorful shower of fat fabric. They fall, settling into an arrangement only a Poodle decorator could appreciate. Restack them; more than likely they'll be tossed up again.

More serious is the other side of Pillow Rights. It's the luxury of softness that is Ike's due. It's the solace of these shared family pillows he has known all his life. It's the craving for them that is sated when with a big sigh—*Uh-huh-h-h-h*—he snuggles down in a stack of them.

A stack ... or a single pillow. One Pillow Right is his people-type use, which generally involves only one. He lies down on his back or his side and places only his head on the pillow—as his people do. On the beds he has a choice: ordinary rights of a stack, or people-use rights on sleeping pillows.

One day after changing the linens on Dave's and my bed—but before I put the bedspread on—I was called to the phone. When I returned I found my fresh pillow case already mussed. It was still being used. Mr. Aroonus was reclining with his black Poodle head resting on my pillow.

That was Ike's doing.

It's our doing when we slip a pillow under his head if he's lying on the couch without one. As if it makes any difference in the extent we go to make a Poodle comfortable, we say—*"Ike* started it, this sleeping with his head on a pillow!"

       *   *   *

And Ike started something else.

He started reminding us of other Aroonus comforts we might overlook in the car.

His Automobile Comfort Rights.

Sometimes Ike's people don't seem to comprehend weather, and temperature, and comforts. It becomes necessary for a Poodle to tell them things like: *Turn on the air conditioner!*

Ike and I were parked at school waiting for Brian one day of our second spring in Texas. It was warm, very warm, a day that was a harbinger of the summer that was to come. I hadn't turned on the air conditioner during the drive to school. In fact, I hadn't used it at all that season. I suppose I hadn't yet switched my thinking from just-right days to hot days.

But Ike had.

He was hot, and he remembered the remedy. But he had to convince me.

He stretched forward and nosed the air conditioner vents. He barked at me.

That did it.

That was the beginning. He had asked and received. He had reminded one of his people with success. Afterward Aroonus the Pampered asked for cool air often. Many times even before the engine was started. Why should he be uncomfortable for a minute longer than need be? Why, indeed, when the flip of a switch brought a jet of air to squint his eyes and lift his ears into Poodle wings.

And to his face it brought a look. Of gratitude? No. The smug look of one accepting what is his.

It's the same look when he finds his freshly laundered bed linens. He climbs into his bed so he can lie there and sniff his mattress and his cover.

He expects clean bed linens. It's one of the Linen Rights of Mr. Aroonus. Like so many of his rights, he has had these a long time. Since that puppy puddling in his bed.

Since the first mud on puppy paws. Time on the box — California rain, California dew — yielded many dirty towels.

As does Dallas rain. Dallas dew. Dallas snow.

Linen Rights. Weather inspired or the result of a bath, the problem of a pile of wet dirty towels is solved by Linen Rights.

Linen Rights make possible a clean afghan...a spotless sweater.

The afghan is kept in the den, but in the utility area, on Ike's shelf — a shelf that is strictly reserved for Poodle use — is where Mr. Aroonus's sweater and his supply of clean towels are stored.

IT'S A LONG SHELF. Whether it is three short shelves like he had in California, or one long shelf, Mr. Aroonus needs ample storage space. For his supplies, his *toiletries*.

Toiletry Right: the right to possess and derive benefit from the various grooming aids necessary for a pampered Poodle.

The right to have an electric clipper and extra blades, three brushes, two combs, a special canine nail file, and a nail trimmer.

And for baths — the bottle of shampoo, a tub sponge, cream rinse, a rubber hose spray.

Cotton balls and cotton swabs for use in ear medication and cleaning. (A Poodle uses more cotton than an entire family.) There are the ear-care bottles: alcohol, canker medicine, ear cream. And a plastic container of ear powder.

Ear care is a right.

So is skin and coat care....

Hence, a bottle of skin medicine (for itching), a coat conditioner spray, a deodorant spray, and a flea and tick spray.

A plastic bowl sits on Ike's shelf. Yes, it's a grooming aid. It's for muddy Poodle paws. It's his foot bath bowl.

     *   *   *

AROONUS RIGHTS... THERE IS ONE MORE. The right to an inexhaustible supply of dog food. But not just any kind. When Ike commands *Give me food*, he asks for Ike's Brand only.

We used to wonder what would happen if we ever ran out of Ike's Brand at a crucial time. It finally happened.

On a Saturday morning, the crucial time came. It was 7:35 A.M. The reason we were up so early on a Saturday quickly became a sorry, tarnished one. Ike banged his bowl for breakfast. For the first time in three years we had run out of Ike's Brand. The grocery stores wouldn't open until 8:30 A.M. Not for 55 minutes.

Fifty-five minutes of intensive pampering.

Fifty-five minutes of disregarding everything but the efforts to pacify an irate Poodle.

We played with him. Ike would stop the game abruptly and bang his bowl — and bark. We gave him goodies. Fine. He ate them, then banged his bowl. And barked. We gave him a new sock. He took it

to his bed and chewed it briefly, then banged his bowl. And barked. We talked to him. We fed him people-food tidbits. We scratched his chest. We rubbed his ears. He banged his bowl. And barked. And looked at the empty spot on the shelf in the pantry.

And looked at us with disgust.

At 8:20 A.M. Dave left for the nearest grocery store. At 8:33 A.M. he was paying the cashier for his purchase of Ike's Brand.

At 8:40 A.M. the banging bowl was stilled...but not completely silent. There was a tinkling sound as Ike's dog tags touched the bowl rim with the rhythm of his eating. He finally had what he wanted. Not talk, not play, not goodies, not chest-scratching, not ear-rubbing, not food tidbits. But placation in the only possible manner—with Ike's Brand.

For Aroonus the Pampered nothing but Ike's Brand....

There is one other possibility we hardly dare think about: What would happen if that food company should ever discontinue Ike's Brand?

IKE LIKES

I Ke's Brand

CHAPTER TEN

IKE'S BRAND IT IS. Ike's Brand it was that first time. We had tried every brand on the grocer's shelf. All the others Ike would half-heartedly eat one time, maybe not at all the next. Then—as if an ad writer were directing the action—we fed Ike's Brand to our puppy. That was it, a wedding of Poodle palate and dog food.

After eating Ike's Brand for three years, he was still just as enthusiastic a proponent.

Ike likes. With Ike it is never a lukewarm preference. His support is total.

He is every bit as selective with his Poodle treats; he is as loyal to his goodies as to Ike's Brand.

But let's face it. Poodle food is fairly limited. Now people food is different. Ah, people food. There are so many good people foods ...like steak smothered in wine sauce with mushrooms. So many kinds other than steak. The hams, turkeys, and roasts that are subjected to the levitation nose.

So many kinds...all worthy of the art of begging. The highly seasoned ones that are fit for a king Poodle. Few foods are better than homemade chili, or tacos, or spaghetti. Ike probably feels he's mistreated when he is given only a few bites of foreign dishes in lieu of a people-size serving.

Some other farfetched canine preferences are the crunchy foods ...like melba toast. Raw celery, green onions, and green pepper. And raw carrots. The entrancing summons of a raw carrot taken from the vegetable crisper is second only to that of meat. But no glutton is Ike when a delectable carrot has been pared, ready to eat. Carrot protocol calls for hand-feeding, with a human hand held under his chin so he doesn't have to take bites to his bed...and dissection into small pieces. No gulping of carrots, but slow, exaggerated mastication that allows time to savor the goodness, and time to appreciate the crunchiness.

What is crunchier than an apple? What is tastier than a Poodle share of the apples his people are eating? Nothing is, at least at the time apples are the only available, likable people food for which to beg.

When Ike first came to us, he found that apples were often served as an evening snack. He learned to be ready and await his share by sitting or lying squarely on a juice-absorbing newspaper. Now he is some six times larger and much neater when eating apple bites, but he still hunts for a newspaper. If one isn't readily accessible, he fidgets and frets like a meticulous bachelor.

Crunch....

The crunch of a green salad. If the dressing is bleu cheese.

The crunch of peanuts. Popcorn. Both held in the highest esteem.

Both declared *equal foods*, which means no small, token portions for Ike, but foods shared *bite for bite*.

You take a bite. Ike takes a bite. You take a bite. Ike takes a bite.

Try to fool him, and take two bites in a row. He nudges you and with eyes wide gives you a look that asks a plaintive: *How could you?*

Peanuts he can eat out of the half shell. The tip of his tongue scoops up the nuts so quickly it's almost impossible to see how he does it.

When sharing people food with us, Ike likes a steady pace. No socializing. No amenities. Only eating...you one bite...Ike one bite. If it's too slow, again he nudges you. *Come on—speed it up.*

A party to Ike is when some of his favorite foods are served and shared in the living room or den. A party can be nothing more than a bowl of potato chips. Or corn chips. Or a tray of crackers and cheese. Or Danish pastry. Or ice cream. Or cookies—especially vanilla wafers.

There is a special food love. Salt water taffy. There's something about it that tantalizes Ike's taste buds. From time to time a box of the taffy comes to us from California friends. They mail it to the family, but I suspect they send it primarily to Ike. That's what Ike thinks, too, for after he takes possession of the package and demands that it be opened, he barks for bites of the taffy he likes so well.

But most foods don't come by mail. Most of them are brought home by Ike's people. On grocery shopping days.

Ike loves grocery days. The food is one reason. But there is another.

The paper sacks in which the food is packed. He barks; he paws at the sacks; he wiggles and turns impatiently until the first sack is emptied.

That one is Ike's. "Okay, it's yours, Ike." He grabs it and with its brown bulk almost obscuring his vision he prances to his bed.

He anchors the sack with his front feet and begins to shred it with his teeth. He works, and works, and works. The powerful tugs cord the muscles of his long neck.

There is no sack limit. He'll take as many as his begging procures, maybe more...if he can steal them.

And he's not above stealing a sack with purchases still in it. If it's light enough to carry in his mouth it's eligible to be an Ike sack.

Nor does it have to be a big grocery sack. Any paper bag will do. Size doesn't seem to influence Ike's delight. The only difference between big sacks and little ones is the time it takes him to do an Ike job on them.

Bits and pieces of brown sack paper pile up in his bed—like freshly raked autumn leaves. Bits and pieces with edges that are ruffled from dog saliva. Bits and pieces lying on the floor around his bed—the overflow.

Sack pleasure is Ike's; the cleaning up is his people's.

But once, as I knelt by his bed to pick up the remains of sack fun, Ike assumed a measure of responsibility. He picked up a sack scrap that had fallen behind his bed and dropped in into my hand.

In the car, too, Ike would like to have sacks. His teasing nibbles have hinted at that desire. We take no chances. We hide little bags under the seat and put big ones in the trunk when Ike is to be left alone in the car.

Even with sack deprivation, to be left alone in the car is not a thing to be dreaded. Quite the opposite.

It's difficult to think back...all the way back...before the car pillow...and remember that tiny, trembling little puppy who didn't like the car.

Now it's not even easy to remember when he preferred to ride in the back seat. One time The Lady, still sweet-smelling after a day with first dirty, then clean Poodles, brought Ike home in her personal car instead of the Poodle van. "You certainly have Ike well trained," she said. "I wanted him to ride in the front seat with me—I coaxed him—but he wouldn't budge from the back." I had to admit it was more his own preference than human discipline. And somewhere along the line he developed that Poodle trait of car seat hopping. Front to back. Back to front. He might be seeking a decision—front?...or back? Or his nervous hopping back and forth might be a car pleasure within itself. It could be. He has a strong attachment to the automobile.

Merely to sit in the car is blissful. For hours if weather permits —if it isn't too hot or too cold. To sit in the car, whether it's still in the garage without having moved an inch, or parked in front of a shop, restaurant, or the school. Anywhere, anytime, Ike is happy in the car.

It beats staying in the house by himself, all alone, away from people and happenings.

Sometimes the car is more than a vehicle of happiness within itself. It can transport a Poodle and his people to places where good things occur. The car can mean picnics.

Ike likes picnics—half-picnics or whole picnics.

In California, at the beach, half-picnics began. No food. Simply a brief time watching the ocean churn into white foam—or into a shadowy maroon when there was a red tide. To sniff constantly was Ike's prerogative. Head lifted. Nose twitching as if there might never be another smell to excite it.

And his ears . . . flexing at the sounds. What did Ike listen to on those half picnics? To the birds—this time the brash sea gulls. To the rumbles of the ocean, to its music-like rhythm. And to the ubiquitous jets as they lifted up over the sea or skimmed down for a landing at L.A. International, the chocolate cake for the sky full of jet ants.

. . . The jets again, at a half-picnic at Bachman Lake in Dallas. This time close enough for Ike to hear the screech and skid of the landings . . . to remind him of his arrival in Texas . . . more facsimiles of his jet trip.

One half-picnic at Bachman was a sack of peanuts shared by Ike and his people—the snap of peanut shells completely obliterated by the takeoffs of the jets. Facing away from us, their upturned rears were like giant ducks expelling clouds of black gas. Giant ducks to bark at.

Half-picnics are minimum.

Whole picnics are maximum. Total. All the way. Water jug, plenty of food, unhampered time—at least the greater part of a day. A whole picnic like Ike's first one. In Dallas, but this time at one of the large secluded lakes, not in the middle of the city like Bachman.

To Ike that first whole picnic meant freedom. No leash. His only space restriction was a generous periphery around the picnic site, the bounds of which surprisingly enough were set by Ike. The area was circumscribed by certain trees. Ike knew each tree that defined that circle...plus every tree inside it, plus every bush, plus every blade of grass.

Every upright bit of vegetation became a hurry spot at least twice during the picnic, some half a dozen times. If the number of hurryings could have sufficed for the following days, Ike wouldn't have needed to hurry again for a month. After so long it was merely a gesture, a half-hearted male Poodle salute to the outdoors.

Quiet, almost complete quiet. The only sounds were ours and the subdued splashings of a calm lake.

Suddenly there was a new sound. Ike stopped—dead still, as dogs have done since time began. One front foot was frozen in midair, the only movement a quiver of his nose.

The sound was repeated. Ike relaxed. He glanced at us, then looked up toward a treetop and whined. There on a high branch sat a mockingbird. Ike's bird at a picnic? Out here in the wilderness?

Water and food are integral parts of a whole picnic. The water jug satisfied Ike's real and imagined thirsts time and time again. He had his own paper cup, and he had a bark that asked for it to be filled with cold water.

Mealtime began a picnic-only custom that was and is especially appealing to Ike. He sat on the bench with us that first picnic and was served his portion from the picnic table.

By the end of the picnic, Ike was filthy. His coat was decorated with outdoor memorabilia of leaves, burrs, twigs, and soil. I drew the tedious job of brushing him before we left the lake. For Ike it was a proper climax to a picnic, the attention that egressed through the brush and comb and the towel dampened with lake water to finish his cleanup.

His first whole picnic had completely exhausted Ike. That night he retired of his own accord before his usual ten o'clock curfew. Any night it's evident that Ike loves his bed, but I know that time he had a special appreciation of it. Secure in his bed, quite possibly he contemplated the joys of the day.

The components of a whole picnic were not forgotten. The next time he saw the picnic basket, the water jug, his brush, the blanket —picnic ecstasy touched him once again.

Ecstasy comes often to a Poodle who overreacts to his many and sometimes bizarre likes.

Likes that are bizarre by people standards but not by Ike's. Take human feet. As long as they perform their duty of locomotion these leg terminals are looked upon with indifference by Ike's people and friends. Not by Ike. To him human feet are lovable catalogs of the owners. And as such, they are due canine admiration and care. How does he show this? He licks them.

Lick. Lick. Lick. When Ike licks feet he has the same look on his face as when he laps an ice cream cone. He likes ice cream. He likes feet, too.

He sees a human foot. The desire to lick may or may not come over him. If it does, Ike is persistent. If his target is moving, he nips at the heel until immobility comes. If the target is clad in either shoes or hose, or both, he paws it . . . not without exasperation. Often he slaps at the shoe- or hose-clad foot he wants to lick and then walks a few feet away. He returns almost immediately to the same foot and looks it over, as if the brief time lapse has suddenly stripped the foot bare.

Clean feet. Dirty feet. He likes both kinds.

Of the family feet, mine are the favored ones. They get the most Ike licking. Availability is one reason — my feet are at home more than Dave's and Brian's, and I often have on slippers and no hose. Another reason is that I'm a somewhat more willing victim.

Then, too, my feet often have the smell of lotions and creams.

More odd likes. Perfumes and scented cosmetics that people wear. I wonder if part of The Lady's initial attraction was her perfume.

Recently a tiny lady visitor, a little girl, was especially interesting to Ike. He licked her cheek. We pulled him away and scolded him. A few minutes later he was at her face again. Once more we scolded him. He was cowed, but something compelled him to return to the pink cheeks. Dave took hold of Ike's collar; that was the only thing that stopped Ike. What was the matter with him? Shortly the explanation came. The mother mentioned casually that she had put lotion on the child's cheeks. And it was Ike's favorite fragrance.

A friendly female guest's aura of perfume is apt to draw Ike to her for a closer inspection. He likes to sniff the places of application — the ear lobes, the neck, the elbows, the knees. When Ike is on a perfume inspection, our explanations hardly seem adequate: "Ike likes perfume." "Ike likes women — and girls."

Ike likes shampoo, too. I don't know whether it's because of the scent. Or the suds. Or both. Or because it's a license to lick. His tongue reaches for the rim of suds that unavoidably forms on the forehead; he never touches the hair. He licks the soap on the brow, and after a quick cleanup of stray blobs of suds on the cheek, an ear, or an eyelid, he's through. That's all. He leaves and doesn't return during that particular shampoo.

For a Poodle that likes bizarre things like feet, and perfume, and shampoo, there's really no limit to his odd preferences. I don't think there will ever be a limit. Not as long as he encounters the new.

Not as long as the new is something like a feather duster.

What is that bunch of feathers? A saucy, turquoise imitation of Ike's bird that flits back and forth across bric-a-brac? Something pretty for which to beg? A personal possession to be carried to his bed and guarded with snarls when his people try to retrieve it? Whatever else it is, to Ike it definitely isn't a dusting tool.

No limit to odd likes. . . .

Gummed tape sets Ike wild. He sees us cutting strips of it for a package, and he pushes in, up, around, and tries to be the official moistener. It's like outmaneuvering an octopus to wrap and seal a package in Ike's presence. He's fascinated by any kind of gummed tape; even used, pre-pasted, dried out, crinkled tape on an old box is almost as desirable as new.

Package wrapping goes no smoother in this house if string is used. Ike likes string better than gummed tape. He was introduced to string when he was a puppy. The liking was developed, in much the same manner a person learns to like a healthful but unappetizing food. Once or twice a week we brought into our California home Dave's shirts from the laundry. In green cardboard boxes they were —tied with string. For many weeks Puppy Ike watched but didn't touch. It was always the same routine. We untied the string, pulled it from the box, put away the shirts, then dropped the box and string into a wastebasket.

One day puppy circumspection ended. Ike lunged and grabbed the string as it was flipped off. To his bed—fast. He was in a hurry to create a soggy, limp, slimy length of string. After that day Ike became a string addict.

A Poodle addict jumps, twirls, rotates, yaps, claws, and craves intensely a bizarre object in sight but out of reach.

A rubber band qualifies, too, as such an object.

And each day there is a rubber band delivered to the front door— stretched around a bonus gift of newspaper.

Rubber band desire is sated as quickly as it's taken between Poodle teeth. Unless there's a willing partner. . . .

Someone to hold the band? Joy. Joy. Joy. A game erupts from barren time. A game made up of cunning and sly attacks and withdrawals, and long daring pulls at the elastic plaything. A black muzzle gets snapped. A hasty retreat. Then a counterattack with deliberate feints, followed by a quick pull. A hand gets snapped. "Ouch!"

A game — the most basic of likes. Any kind of game. A true game like retrieving a ball. Or the merest suggestion of a game. Something that repeated once or twice brings pleasure.

Or a crazy kind of Ike game. Not with his people. With some queer little Dallas bugs.

Little brown bugs that attracted by the patio lights come by the tens on a warm summer evening. They fall from the air, land on their backs, making tiny thuds on the concrete. Ike selects one of many and gently carries it off to the edge of the patio to release it and watch it jump up and land on its back. After a few jumps the bug reposes. Ike goes after another, takes it to a different spot and watches this one until it tires. Again ... he gets another bug ... carefully ... always carefully. He's never anything but gentle with his little brown bugs.

Ike Dislikes

CHAPTER ELEVEN

WITH CALIFORNIA SNAILS Ike was never anything but deadly.

But the individual snail did have some measure of choice as to its own fate. If it made its sluggish route *away* from the area of Ike's chain it didn't face immediate destruction. It might, as many did, crawl to the house, climb up the exterior wall and there leave a shiny glazed spot on the plaster. Or it might make its way to the flowers and dine. But if the snail chose to creep inside Ike's circle, it was doomed.

Ike disliked those grayish mollusk pests. The moment he spied one he moved in for the unique kill.

He'd lower his nose directly above the snail. There was no hurry, not with a languid snail. Ike would watch it...until the time was right. Then Ike snaked in. Starting with the tip of his muzzle, he slid his entire head — and only his head, not any part of his body — over the snail. He had to repeat this head slide several times before the snail was dead inside its crushed shell.

We always knew when Ike had killed a snail. His face reeked of an offensive, musty odor. The only remedy was soap and water. It could have been worse — if he had slid his body over the eventually squashy mollusk.

Why did Ike dislike snails? Because they trespassed on his personal ground? Because of their smell? Their slow pace? The look of them? The cowardly shell?

And what does a stick pretzel have in common with a snail?

We were sure Ike would like pretzels. Doesn't he like crunchy snack foods?

I extended my hand and offered him his first pretzel. His nose — an eighth of an inch away — vibrated as he took a sixty-second case history of this strange object. He formed an opinion.

He took the pretzel, dropped it on the floor, and gave it his snail treatment. On his side, he slithered a few inches so he could slide his head across the pretzel. He got up. He sniffed the pretzel. Then he slid on it again. Another sniff. Another slide. Again, and again, and again.

Why couldn't he crush the shell of this strange snail?

"Ike, look. It's food. See?"

Dave ate a pretzel to show him. But Ike would have no part of our escargot fare. He slid once again on the long slender Texas counterpart of a California snail.

Regardless of the category in which Ike puts pretzels, they are nevertheless a disliked *food*.

There are other disliked foods, too. Sherbet is one. Strange ... he relishes ice cream and yet despises sherbet. A full bowl of sherbet — any flavor — doesn't deserve so much as a lifted brow.

Another ... hot cakes made from ready-mix. A dastard attempt to fool a Poodle who thinks highly of Mommer's own hot cakes.

Hot cakes, if you please. No synonyms like griddle cakes. Or flapjacks. Or even pancakes. Ike recognizes only hot cakes. And it's a very literal meaning. If they're hot, they're hot cakes.

If they're cold, they are worse than hot cakes made from a mix. Cold hot cakes are not worthy of a fork — says gourmet Ike with his actions — and are to be abhorred.

One morning for the first time we were told of our puppy's loathing for cold hot cakes. Ike refused this already favorite tidbit. We had deliberately waited for his bites to cool this time because we had discussed the danger of giving a puppy hot food.

Ike kept returning to the cold bites. He wouldn't eat, but he seemed to want to.

We decided to test him. I heated the bites of hot cakes.

He gobbled them up.

Nothing about this food has changed since then. Please remember ... *hot* hot cakes ... remember....

Remember something else, too. Ike's food and water bowls. Wash them by hand. It takes too long in the dishwasher.

Surely I'm not foolish enough to believe a Poodle can get by during all that dishwasher time without water—and without the comfort of seeing his food bowl?

Sometimes I am that foolish and torment Ike by letting the dishwasher do his dishes. He, in turn, torments me. He barks for water once, twice, maybe three times and gets his interim drinks from a paper cup.

I know he dislikes having his bowls out of sight.

When they are, it is therefore my fault. I force this dislike upon him. His retribution is to make me serve him. And quite often ordinary tap water isn't sufficient emollient for the agony of his dislike. What he needs is cold water. He stands at the refrigerator door and barks for *picnic* water.

My fault. Guilty I may be for washing Poodle bowls incorrectly, but some things are not my fault. Things like rain.

That November day there was a cloudburst. The kind of heavy rain Texas calls a gully washer. In the middle of it Ike wanted out.

"It's raining too hard, Ike." I took him to the window. "See?" He knew it was raining, but that day he preferred proof before acknowledgment of a weather problem.

He simply had to go out. His barks said it was an emergency. A dire threat-to-the-floor emergency. I relented. When I opened the back door, it was like looking at the back side of a waterfall. Ike pushed out, squinting his eyes shut. A two-foot advance was enough. He returned.

A toweling-down for Ike. And for me. A floor-mopping.

And an angry Poodle. Ike ran to the den window. He barked at me. My fault because his mission had failed?

Five minutes later Ike wanted out. Again? "It's still raining, Ike." *Bark. Bark. Bark.*

This time it took five feet of outdoors to convince him, and when he came back I *knew* he blamed me.

He growled as I toweled his wet coat. He barked. He ran through the house. He skidded on throw rugs. He scooped up his ball on a dead run and when he released it it bounced upon a table and over-turned a candle and holder. Still running, he picked up his house bone and tossed it into the air. When he stopped at last, he was directly in front of me. Facing me, he barked again and again.

My fault. Why didn't I stop the heavy rain? Didn't I know Ike disliked it? Couldn't I at least slow it down to the gentle rain he liked?

Ike dislikes hard rain . . . he dislikes thunderstorms.

A Texas storm, perhaps, points out a similarity to the Fourths of July, with an exception. A storm's duration is shorter than a Fourth. But it's long enough.

Too long.

The great cloud masses last too long. The driving rain lasts too long. The eerie blackness that pushes daylight aside lasts too long. The wind with a fury that bends trees to the ground lasts too long. The quick little respites of calmness don't last long enough. The pounding hail lasts too long. The lightning flashes that vein the sky in yellow last too long.

Too long — the gustiness, the wildness, the cacophony.

Ike hates all the storm noises, but most of all he dislikes the sound of thunder. He barks at each clap. Wherever he is, he barks: on the floor, standing on our feet (to get as close as possible), or in our arms.

Being held is the best, particularly during the blackest and noisi-est part of a storm. When we put him down he whines and tries to climb back up.

Not only does he bark at the thunder. Now and again he growls. Barking alone cannot express his complete disapproval and fear when thunder rolls and cracks on our very rooftop.

A spring storm is soon spent. Its going relaxes Ike. It leaves him wiser, a little more experienced in the way of storms and their sounds...it's a wise Poodle that profits from experiences with sounds.

There was another sound one day, and maybe to Puppy Ike it was like a tiny thunderclap. *Thump*. A baseball hit his head. He yelped. Why shouldn't he. It was a surprise pain.

He had been minding his own business, investigating parts of the yard he couldn't reach from his chain. He was running free because he wasn't alone; Dave and Brian were playing catch in the backyard. Ike was sniffing under a fuchsia bush, reviewing maybe the route of a snail or a gopher—when the ball hit him.

All the human attention—the head rubbing, the verbal soothing, the apologies—perhaps alleviated the pain. But it didn't erase the memory of this new dislike. After that the sight of Dave and Brian with baseball gloves sent Ike under a chair or a bed. He could not be persuaded to go outside. Then, after we moved, he either became braver or else he decided the Dallas yard was safer for Poodle baseball spectators.

At any rate, he would stay in the yard during a game of catch—until another fateful baseball day. Ike was standing at the fence, peering through a hole when a fast ball slipped by Brian.

Crack. It hit the fence a couple of inches above Ike's head. The startled jump and the yelps proclaimed it might as well have been Ike's head again instead of the fence.

That did it. The game of catch would never have another chance to be anything but a *dislike*. Never again would he stay in the yard to hear that *crack* on the fence or worse yet, his head.

From that time on, all he wanted was the *thump* of the door as it closed between a game of catch and him.

Thump—that's a pleasant sound when it's a door closed because Ike wishes it. The thump when the door closes him off each night, and when he's to be left alone...so be it. But that *thump* when one of us shuts him out for no legitimate reason—that's a dislike. (Could it be that Dave started it the time he playfully tricked Ike and closed him out of the bedroom?)

Thump. Regardless of where he is in the house, that sound is a door slammed in his face. *Thump*. Someone has ruined his egress and ingress. *Thump*. His dislike is born anew.

That door must be opened. An Ike attempt is first. He pushes if the door swings in. With a paw he tries to pull it open if it swings out. And he knows which way every house door swings.

That door must be opened. It must be. If Ike can't do it alone, he knocks. Of course, in truth he scratches, but when Ike scratches it's like a knock. A scratch...then an interval...another scratch...another interval...then louder...he waits...still louder. (He knocks when he wants to come in from the yard, but the difference is that after a while outdoor knocking includes barking, too.)

As soon as his knocking reaches maximum intensity—a measurement adjudged by Ike—he holds it at that degree until one of several things happens: The person behind the door admits Ike and shuts the door again, in which case Ike may start the whole thing again on the other side—because he wants the door left open. Or the person yields to Ike completely and loses all privacy. Or his other people persuade Ike to stop knocking (unlikely) or else remove him bodily from the scene, and hold him bodily to keep him away. Or while at the shut door Ike hears a sound that draws him to another part of the house. An important sound.

Perhaps the *thump* of another door.

Or the different sound of another dislike, for example—the upright vacuum cleaner.

That roaring cyclops that glides and rotates and swerves all through the house, bent on devouring Poodles. But it can be outsmarted. It can be outmaneuvered. It can be outrun.

It can be outvoiced by a Poodle's incessant barking.

There is bedlam in the Lusk house when I start the vacuum cleaner. Barking loudly and shrilly, Ike gallantly defends his home and people, courageously makes passes at the cyclopean monster, nips at its distended bag.

Thank goodness, the Poodle courage wanes after a time. The lure of the battle no longer activates Ike. Then I can do my housework in peace while Ike seeks refuge in the office under the desk or on Dave's and my bed. The battle instinct is revived briefly when he hears me putting the cleaner away. Warrior Ike barks it into the closet. Until the next time the vacuum cleaner is silent. But not Ike.

Not a vocal dog like Ike.

There are still other sounds he must answer. Other sounds that need his barks of disapproval.

There are the sounds of the paper boy and the postman. When the newspaper is thrown against the house, or the mailbox lid is dropped, Ike tears through the house toward Brian's room. He skids around corners. He pours out savage cries like his wild ancestors. At Brian's door Ike begins his leap and lands in the middle of the bed. From there he can see. From there he angrily barks at the paper boy or the postman.

They each commit the vilest of acts: They hit Ike's house. Once daily Ike accuses and tells the paper boy to mend his ways. The postman isn't so lucky; Ike tells him three times daily. The first when the mailman deposits the mail.

Then Ike waits at Brian's window until the postman works his way down the block and up again across the street. A second chance for Ike to bark. *You'd better not hit our house again.* Still Ike waits. He issues the third warning when the red, white, and blue mail car goes by.

The paper boy and the postman both ignore Ike's admonishments. But Ike never gives up.

Nor does he give up telling off motorcycle riders. They don't irritate Ike by hitting the house, but their noise — the deafening chug and whine of their cycle motors — is just as heinous a crime.

Ike hears a motorcycle in the distance. Up he springs. Another run for Brian's bed. Barking all the way. Barking when he is stationed on the bed. Tail straight up like a pointed finger emphasizing each bark. *Get a bicycle, you noisemakers! Beware of this house.*

In the car Ike is rankled by motorcycle riders, too. He barks a warning — even snarls and bares his teeth if they come too close.

In the car there is one circumstance that prevents his trying to reform motorcycle enthusiasts, when he is too wrapped up in another dislike. This is when he is *downtown.*

Ike doesn't like downtown. He cries. He whines. He moves from side to side on the car seat like a restless, caged animal. He acts this way until downtown is left behind.

Why does he dislike it?

Downtown is traffic. Traffic is noise. But traffic and its noise are everywhere—in the suburbs, on the freeways, in the shopping centers. His dislike isn't because of the noise alone. It isn't the traffic alone.

Downtown is buildings, but the downtowns Ike dislikes aren't made up of exceedingly tall buildings. His dislike isn't because of high rise alone.

Downtown is people tension. And people tension can mean Poodle tension. But driving anywhere can cause taut nerves. His dislike isn't because of tension alone.

Why does Ike dislike downtown? It could be a combination of all these things. And on the other hand, it may not be any of them. Perhaps the answer is something people couldn't understand....

And people actually understand very little about a complicated animal like Ike. I can't even explain why he doesn't like to be sprayed. He loves people perfumes, hair sprays, and cosmetics; yet he runs and hides when he sees one of his spray cans taken from his shelf. Even his dog cologne spray.

Neither can I explain why he dislikes male hats but has no

objection to female head coverings. Is it because he likes female strangers better than male strangers? Or does he dislike male strangers *because* of male hats?

Is it because of this incident? Puppy Ike was fastened on his chain when two little boys—each wearing a hat—slipped up, from the corner of the house, upwind, and startled Ike. Then they tried to rush him into play. From the kitchen window I saw his fear turn to menace, and I ran outdoors to intervene. Could this have caused a lifelong hatred of hats? And only male hats? Can a puppy equate little boys with adult men?

Whatever the reason, a strange man is always suspect. If he wears a hat and wants Ike as a friend he has a problem. One hat-wearing, dog-loving, family friend tried for over a year to win Ike over. Ike would never go to him. What would happen if the friend stopped wearing a hat? With Ike is it *once a hat always a hat?*

It isn't logical that Ike should shun the prospect of a staunch friend after so long a time. In spite of a hat.

No, it isn't logical.

At least it is an illusive logic when subjected to human explanation. However, there is some kind of basis for each thing Ike likes or dislikes. That basis is the canine logic.

And in the case of Ike—it is his own logic.

CHAPTER TWELVE

HIS OWN CANINE LOGIC.

A sometimes opaque reasoning...as it was one evening when Ike had gone to the bedroom with me. His relaxed position on the bed indicated he was content, but suddenly he left. In a few minutes he returned with Dave. "He pawed at my arm," Dave said, "and brought me back here. Did you send him?" No. Ike had sent himself; and now he settled down once again—*Uh-huh.*

Why did he for no obvious reason bring Dave to the bedroom?

Ike knew why. Numerous human conjectures might or might not uncover the real answer. But let Ike have his mental secrets. At least some of his logic is clear enough for his people to understand.

Could it be any clearer than this?

My transistor radio was on the coffee table. I had been listening to it in the garage while stripping an old piece of furniture, and when I came into the house I set it on the table. It was still playing, rather loudly. Ike walked up to it and stood there for a moment listening to the music. Next he walked slowly to one of the wall speakers and stopped. He listened. No sound. Then he went to the other stereo speaker. He listened. No sound. Then back to the coffee table. He cocked his head to one side. The sound shouldn't be here. It should come from the big speakers.

Ike thinks...and the results are there.

Thinking is cataloging information that at some future time will be part of a deduction. Information about such things as a new pair of pants for Dave. *Oh, new pants!* Ike begins to sniff the moment he sees them, sniffs the pants as Dave pulls them on. The Poodle nose works like something mechanical as long as the Poodle brain needs this kind of information. Suddenly he has gleaned enough smell information. Ike sits back waiting because there is more cataloging to come. Yet needed is the answer to what *kind* of pants are these. Ike has to watch, see what Dave does when completely dressed. Will these be office pants? Woodworking-in-the-garage pants? Yard pants? *Going* pants? Whatever Dave does next will establish the answer for Ike. Then the next time Dave wears this pair of pants Ike will know the kind of activity that will be forthcoming.

Thinking is making a decision. Give Ike an alternative. He knows how to make a choice.

Repeatedly he blocks the bathroom door when I'm ready to shower. "Do you want to come in here with me, or do you want to stay in the bedroom?" I ask him. No rash decision... he takes his time . . . he likes to deliberate. He looks first one way, then the other.

You can almost *see* the process of his thinking. Which will be his choice? In? Or out? Bathroom? Or bedroom? The decision varies, but it's his decision. He wants to choose. He wants to be *asked*.

And when he is asked beforehand, he respects the closed door. It's the only time he doesn't hate the *thump* as a door is shut.

An informed dog accepts, and that which is accepted becomes routine.

Frequently his people can inform Ike. An example is when we plan to go somewhere without Ike. In advance we tell him — "Ike will stay. Ike will go to bed." He knows. He understands the *stay*: it means our early preparations to go are indicative of only our pleasure to be — not Ike's. He understands the *go to bed*: that's his starting station when he's left alone.

But there are some things you can't explain to a dog.

When his people cannot inform Ike, when the situation is too difficult, Ike depends upon his own logic. Ike logic tells him what he needs to know. Ike logic tells him the answer.

Tells him the answer to aborted routine.

An answer that is sought when one of his people doesn't come home. An answer that is desperately sought when his instinct singles out certain emotions of his other people.

Ike was six months old when Dave was ill in the hospital. Those first few days Ike didn't answer the phone during his telephone hour. Even before he found the reason for Dave's absence, this much he already knew: Dave wasn't at work . . . and wouldn't or couldn't call us for his daily pickup. At that point, perhaps Ike wondered if Dave would ever return to us. Perhaps he was trying to reconcile that loss. Perhaps he was experiencing puppy grief. . . .

For the first four or five days Dave wore hospital garments. Then he began to wear his own pajamas. The first time that I brought home a soiled pair of pajamas to launder, Ike had his answer.

Brian held Ike so I could at least get inside the door and be all set for an Ike welcome. Ike saw the plastic pajama bag in my hand and tore away from Brian. He jumped up and grabbed the bag, pulled it to the floor. He pushed his nose into it, rooted around in the folds of the cloth. He sniffed wildly, loudly. Violent snorts that blew his nose. It was as though he couldn't believe what his senses were beginning to reveal. Still burying his nose in the pajamas, which were now half out of the plastic bag, Ike commenced to make a noise, a cross between a whimper and a bark. His tail, which had been erect and stiff, now wagged.

Uncertainty vanished. Ike's own logic had finally convinced him. Wherever Dave was, he hadn't completely left his family. The soiled laundry was a message from Dave.

Each day thereafter Ike eagerly awaited the pajama communication. And then, after the weeks of waiting, Ike received a different message. I brought Dave home from the hospital.

It was the first time I have ever seen a dog do a double take. At first Ike only glanced at Dave; he concentrated on welcoming me. Then came recognition. He looked again... *Dave! It's Dave! It's Dave! It's Dave!*

The waiting was over. Ike yelped and leaped into Dave's arms.

Ike stayed by Dave's side the remainder of the day. Now and then he would smell Dave's face and lick a cheek.

Occasionally now family routine is broken when Dave or perhaps Brian, is away overnight. Ike doesn't approve. He is visibly tense, listens with ears cocked to every street sound, is alert to each phone call (Is it a contact with the missing family member?), is hesitant about retiring at night while the family is divided. What is his logic telling him? Does he still remember Dave's hospital time? Is he afraid each absence is serious? He prefers the kind of family roll call when everyone answers "Here."

He prefers the old familiar pattern.

A pattern that allows only small deviations from the established ... new little procedures that can even become routine themselves.

A routineer not afraid of little changes — that's the paradoxical Ike. But no big, serious variations. No one in the hospital. No one out of town.

Everyone home. That's Ike preference. That's ordinary routine. Everyone home at the usual time, too. That's ordinary routine.

And everyone leaving at the usual time. That's morning routine, and it begins before breakfast when Ike returns to his bed and if chilled demands his Cover Rights.

Morning routine is waiting for a pre-breakfast goody (a "Good morning" gift) from each of us. And then after the people breakfast tidbits, routine is lying there in his bed, watching Brian's feet while Brian sacks his lunch. Waiting... watching... secure in the knowledge Brian will remember. Vanilla wafers for Brian's lunch. And one cookie each morning for Ike. Brian's feet bring it over. Without fail.

Routine may demand that Ike leave his bed now — if it is Brian Ike wants to serve his breakfast. Ike bangs his bowl and barks. (Just a couple of quick bites — he'll eat the rest later.)

Then a little later, still during Mommer and Popper coffee time, morning routine is hearing Brian open the blinds in his room. That sound is one of the last things. Time draws nearer. The showdown is coming.

And then it's a quarter to eight. Pressure is on. Time is at hand.

Maybe another quick bite of his food; it's pressure food. When it's about twelve minutes to eight, routine demands he bark at Dave.

Once Dave leaves the table Ike jumps at him and barks. He follows Dave, heeling, and he gives Dave's hands and feet little warning pseudo-nips.

Ike barks. *Hurry, Dave. Hurry.* Ike pushes; he begs; he hopes. The showdown is here.

Leave, Dave. Now. Go. He glances down the hall. *Leave, Dave — before Brian comes from his room!*

The showdown.

There's logic at work. If Dave leaves alone, if Ike can get him to leave by himself, it means that I will drive Brian to school. And if I drive Brian to school, Ike will get to go. But if Dave takes Brian, then Ike's morning routine is minus a car trip.

Each morning Ike tries to get rid of Dave in time. The showdown. Most of the time Ike loses, because Brian comes from his room in time, ready to ride with Dave.

Ike gives a few barks of disappointment then looks at me. Ready for more routine... he and I go to the door to see Dave and Brian off. Ike stands in front of me, on his hind feet. I hold his forepaws in my hands. Thus we stand, the two of us, until the car is out of sight.

Ike accepts each morning's outcome. Besides, tomorrow there will be another morning routine, another chance to bark Dave away in time, another chance to take Brian to school. But first there's the remainder of today's routine. There's the postman, the paper boy, the food, the sleep, the bossing, the pampering, the playing. And there is the other *going*, other car trips, both the routine and the unexpected.

The unexpected going—a proper spot for the use of his own logic. Even when he doesn't catch the word *go* in our conversation, when it isn't the routine time for an established going, he somehow gets the feeling of a trip in the offing. No one has yet said "You'll stay, Ike. You'll go to bed," so there is hope.

He is watchful. For every sign and nuance. His own logic is at work.

One of his people picks up sunglasses. Ike is up. He barks. He asks. *May I go?*

Just as logic told him a long time ago that sunglasses mean outdoors, so did it tell him a coat or wrap means the same thing. If I'm sewing and try on a jacket, Ike is immediately ready. *Bark. Bark. Bark. Let's go.* A coat is a coat if finished or unfinished. If I am chilled and slip a sweater around my shoulders, Ike is ready then, too.

Logic tells him the purpose of keys. The jingle of keys means *car* and *go*.

Logic tells him to wheedle an invitation. If I rattle keys, Ike barks and goes to my purse. He claws at it.

A possibility of going... canine logic tells Ike to heel, every minute, so he will not miss any of the advance preparations. Logic tells him to run to a door and bark to inform us of his desire to go.

Once it's established we *are* going, and there has been no "You'll stay, Ike," logic tells him not to accept a goody—even as a reward for doing something as told. Why? Because we give him a goody when we put him to bed and leave him. If he takes a goody prior to going, it might mean he'd have to give up the trip and go to bed.

He walks on his hind feet, pulls at us like a little boy begging to be picked up. Logic tells him that once he is in our arms with his head locked around a human shoulder, he has added insurance. We can't leave without him then.

When we take him with us in the car his own logic continues, for wherever Ike is, there, too, is his thinking—going full power—ready to catalog vital information. He may be somewhat relaxed, certain of the exact route we will take. Suddenly there is a switch of directions, a departure from the usual route. Attention. Watch. Absorb new directions. His eyes widen. His neck stretched long, he sits so straight he almost tilts backward. He jerks his head from side to side. The Poodle brain is recording impressions, landmarks, sights, smells he will know the next time.

In the car...thinking, always thinking. Moving, or parked, he searches out the things to weigh, contemplate, and try to understand.

Waiting at the school one day there was a little boy and his mother in the car ahead. The child, about five or six years old, was allowed to leave the car and play close by. Ike watched him constantly. Each time he wandered too far away from the car, Ike barked persistently. The little boy climbed upon the trunk of the car, and his mother showed no concern. Ike did; he barked louder than before.

His own logic tells Ike about the danger when two automobiles almost collide. I know of no wreck he has seen; it has to be canine logic to make him freeze with eyes locked on the scene.

From the car Ike barks at babies. Whether they're in cars or being carried by women walking down the street, Ike barks at them. Maybe it is his own logic again, telling him babies and Poodles have something in common: they're both carried so often by their people.

Logic tells Ike to smell our breaths when we return to the parked car to see if we ate anything while we were gone.

When the car is moving, logic tells Ike when to rise up and look out the rear window, when to brace.

Logic tells him the clicking of the turn indicator means a turn—so he braces. Familiar street—unfamiliar street. Relaxed—tense. Ike watches constantly. Watches the driver's feet and their pedal action. Watches the road and its periphery. He sees every stop sign. He braces when he sees one. Braces before deceleration, before a foot goes to the brake pedal. Only once did we see him make a mistake. He thought a school zone sign was a stop sign. The two are similar in color and shape. Is his sign logic based on color? (Dogs are supposed to be color-blind.) Based on shape? Is it because signs are at the side of the road?

He knows traffic signal lights, too. And they're not always the same shape. Most often they hang overhead and have, of course, different colors.

When Ike sees a traffic signal turn red, he braces. When it's green, he doesn't.

Dave drives a red Volkswagen. When Ike and I are in our car and pass a VW, Ike doesn't give it a second glance. Unless it is red. Then it gets a good long look and a brief tail wagging until Ike decides it isn't Dave's car after all.

Poodles are color-blind. If they are, then Poodle logic must explain it. Just plain, common Poodle logic, minus any complicated vision analyses and syllogisms.

It's simple. Ike knows. Logic tells him. Tells him that all Dallas city trucks, regardless of size or kind, are of the same genre as the garbage trucks that come down the alley.

If there is a Poodle who knows what a garbage truck is, it's Ike. It is part of the routine three mornings a week to watch for the orange truck that makes all the stops in the alley behind our house. Ike hates the clang of the cans and lids and barks his hate to the men who do the work. When he is in the house, he watches from the den window. Like an ugly orange bug the truck opens a vast door to its smelly entrails and takes in more refuse.

Later, from Brian's window Ike spots the truck in the next alley. All he can see is a portion of the truck's top—a thin orange line above the trees.

It's logical Ike would recognize and bark at a garbage truck any-where, even when we pull up beside one at a stop sign. But he doesn't quit with the garbage trucks. His own logic prompts him to bark at *any* orange vehicle that belongs to the City of Dallas—whether it be a pickup, a street sweeper, a maintenance truck, a dirt-moving vehicle, or a city tractor.

One day we passed a beige cement truck. Ike spied it, stiffened, all set to bark. Then he turned away, as if he were embarrassed. It was evident he thought at first it was a city truck. What changed his mind? The beige color? (Poodles are color-blind.) The missing "City of Dallas" on the door? (Poodles can't read.)

Or Poodle logic?

On garbage pickup mornings I try to see that Ike is indoors. If he's in the yard his fussing at the city employees and equipment starts a chain of barking that includes almost every backyard in our block, plus several surrounding blocks. I think Ike must be the only canine hater of garbage trucks in the area. He is always the one to start the barking. And his hate is intensified when he is outdoors. Not until there is nothing left of the big orange bug but a faint dis-tant engine roar is Ike free to pursue other routine yard matters... like taking an inventory of the current insect population or check-ing the condition of the hurry bushes and trees.

If it's winter—when the lawn is the color of sand—and if Ike thinks he is due a brushing, logic tells him something to do: Roll in the dead grass. Roll over and over and over. Snake along on your back, feet waving in the air—then on each side. Slide your face and ears through the brittle, scratchy grass.

Ike listens to his logic. He rolls. He rolls until he is transformed into a straw dog. He rolls until he looks like the lawn. No black Poodle now. Gone is the black that looks even blacker contrasted to the greige lawn.

No black Poodle—just the straw dog who has obeyed his own logic. And for a reason of personal pleasure.

Ike knocks. When I open the back door, I behold the straw dog. He looks up at me through grass eyelashes—his face framed by a grass beard—and (no one can convince me otherwise) he grins. *Now you'll brush me!*

I either brush him or leave him outdoors to plague me with con-stant knocking. My limited choice is: I can brush now or later.

I brush. Slowly. Tediously. I remove the many bits of grass liter-ally woven into his coat. I brush and tell him over and over, "Ike, there's an easier way to tell me you need brushing." I can't be too

angry. If I brush him often enough he doesn't roll in the grass. However, I do resent his asking for a goody reward for *letting* me brush
him.

It's late spring, or summer, or early fall, and the lawn isn't dead.
It's virid. If Ike's people are outdoors he likes to have his water

bowl brought to the yard. People logic isn't the same as Poodle
logic, so we don't always do this. When we are negligent, Ike asks
often to be let in for a drink. And unless Brian and Dave are playing
catch, Ike wants to be assured of a return to the yard. Logic tells him
how to handle the situation. He barks for one of us to go inside with
him to his bowl and stand beside him while he drinks. If we walk
away, he barks us back. According to his logic, he can't be left indoors if he keeps one of his people close by.

Proximity and logic. They blend well also at meat tidbit time.
True, he's Boss Ike when he demands — but logic tells him *when*
to demand. Logic tells him to lie down quietly close to the table,
or under it, during our meal. Logic tells him to relax, even take
a nap.

I get up, go to the kitchen. Logic tells Ike: not yet. I return. Then
Dave may serve a food. Or Brian. Not yet, Ike. Then, maybe coffee,
or dessert. Not yet, Ike.

When it is meat tidbit time, when the first chair is pushed back
at the end of the meal, logic says: Now, Ike.

Logic tells him it's time to demand, to boss. And logic never
speaks until *everyone* has finished eating.

And, of course, it is a basic, rudimentary logic that makes it clear his people must dine before any after-dinner meat tidbits can be forthcoming.

Hence, logic makes it permissible for Ike to bark us to the table sometimes when we're dawdling.

Ike knows when dinner is about ready. Most of the signs are obvious. He needs only a tiny bit of logic to know what activities like setting the table mean. And routine long ago established the fact that his people usually dine together.

Therefore, when Dave hasn't come home, Ike knows we'll wait, even though dinner appears to be ready. When logic tells him it is surely almost time for Dave, Ike may bark to go out, because now and then he likes to greet Dave in the backyard. It may be at the direction of his logic once again....

If he meets Dave in the yard, for a few moments there is no sharing of Dave. Ike has his Popper completely to himself for hello time.

And Ike *is* jealous.

Jealousy is one of the many facets of the whole Poodle, the individual Poodle.

The Individual

CHAPTER THIRTEEN

IKE IS JEALOUS. He's jealous of his people, envious of that which we give to each other—our love, our attention, our care. Jealous when he thinks *he* should be receiving instead of observing. Jealous of the three of us as a family unit, engaged in an activity.

For example, that first game of table tennis in the garage. Running from one end of the table to the other became boring to Ike; it was a canine adjunct to the game and certainly not the same as actually playing as his people were. So he tried something else. He chased the ball, but his people ruled that out after the first time. Accustomed to the resistance of a live rubber ball, his powerful jaws crushed the featherweight ball.

Ike didn't seem to mind losing the privilege of chasing the table tennis ball. He probably felt a ball that made a *plink* instead of a *thump* wasn't much of a plaything anyway. Especially one that after a single meeting with Poodle teeth looked like one of those Christmas tree ornaments after he stepped on it.

But now what did Ike have left in the way of table tennis participation? Nothing...except resentment...and a plan.

Only two of his people played at once. The third sat on a stool

137

and watched the game. Until Ike initiated his plan. After that, the
third sat on a stool, watched the game — and held Ike.

Jealous of the three of us.

Jealous of one of us. Of Brian. Jealous of Brian's attention to the
birds. One day from the den window Ike watched Brian put seed in
the bird feeder. Ike watched the almost-tame birds perched close
by. Just as Brian turned to leave, a sparrow nearly touched his
shoulder as it landed on the feeder.

While staring at the scene, Ike must have thought Brian was
giving the birds care and attention that should have been Ike's
alone, because when Brian returned to the house Ike met him with
love. Extravagant love. He rubbed against Brian's legs, then stood
up on his rear feet, looked intently at Brian. Jealousy made him ask,
beg for reassurance from Brian.

Jealous of two of us.

After doing 100 sit-ups in physical education class, Brian had
aching muscles. I was giving him a quick massage. Ike stood in
Brian's doorway, marking well our people conspiracy of attention
against him. He barked. I finished, and Ike — with a twisting walk
and backward glances — asked me to follow him. I did. All the way
to his bed. He climbed in, lay down, rolled over on his back, and
looked at me. I understood the look. I rubbed his tummy and chest
for a moment. With not a vestige of jealousy left, in a happy trot
he then went back to Brian's room.

If Ike is in a certain mood, a people card game can make him
jealous. Dave and I were playing gin rummy on the couch. The
middle cushion was the board. Ike sat at a distance observing, listening, deciding after some time that we were having too much
enjoyment at the exclusion of Ikus P.Q.R.S. Aroonus. When he
could tolerate it no longer he came over, put a tentative foot on
the middle cushion, then another. He climbed up slowly, stiffly.
Would he be pushed back? Would he be told to leave? Dave and I
were as tolerant that day as he was not. For about fifteen minutes
the size of our playing board was reduced by the size of one
Poodle curled up in a ball, his face so close to the game each played
card fanned the feathering on his ears.

There are things worse than gin rummy.

When Dave and I sit too close, Ike pushes between us. And lap-
sitting should be positively forbidden. I shouldn't sit in Dave's lap.
Unless, of course, the lap-sitting includes Ike, too. Which it sometimes does — if there's any lap-sitting at all.

But the offense far worse than sitting together, worse than

lap-sitting is *kissing*. With one exception — when Dave comes home each day — a kiss makes jealousy spring up instantly. Even if it's just a peck, that's all it takes for Ike to act.

Barks. Yelps. Ike jumps at us, between us. Nips at our hands, Claws us. This is what a kiss starts.

And that's what quickly ends a kiss.

But not the aftereffects. If Ike is vulnerable and feels the wrong of our kiss must be righted, then he seeks revenge. We must *pay*. Ike must avenge himself.

There are ways. He may run to his food bowl and bang it repeatedly with a forepaw that emphasizes anger. Once it's filled, he may demand water, or a goody. He may get his sock or a rag and shake it furiously as if it is a thing alive but closer to death with each shake. When it has been shaken enough, it is ready for the play session that revenge allows. A tug-of-war with the major kiss offender — Dave.

Another shape of Poodle vengeance . . . I remember a time in California. Ike had a huge beach ball that because of its size required a special kind of play. He would crook his neck slightly and butt the ball, the arc of his neck and a shoulder making a perfect fit around it. With a lopsided run, he would push the ball at an incredible speed through the house. It was a frantic, discordant kind of Poodle madness. Barks, growls, skids, bumps, and sometimes crashes as he ran the ball into a piece of furniture. That particular day I had seen and heard enough of that wild play. I took the beach ball into the kitchen. Pointing a finger first at the ball, then at Ike, I said, "Play with the ball in here. Stay. Stay." He obeyed me. He did stay. But he barked for me to join him. I had to play ball with him in the kitchen.

Poodle vengeance. Punish the offender. Make him suffer. Ike was tracking a smell in the pantry, stretching, stretching, trying to reach the source. Brian came to his assistance and lifted Ike up. Brian bent over, and Ike — not realizing Brian's grip was still firm — thought he was about to be dropped. He clawed Brian.

Brian's temper flared. He thrust Ike suddenly to the floor, jarring Ike almost as much as the fall would have. Brian stalked off, but he was to return momentarily.

Ike called him back. In one of his favorite retributive ways. He banged his food bowl. Brian answered, "I'm not."

Ike banged again.

Brian said, "No."

Ike banged once more.

Brian returned. "Okay, Ike, I'll give you food if you won't claw me again." He filled the bowl with Ike's Brand. "There. Now eat."

A brief cursory look at the food — not even so much as a smell — and Ike walked away.

The offenders deserve the outcome.

It was bedtime, and Dave had propped a yard chair against the mimosa trunk, Ike's favorite night hurry spot. Three times Ike sniffed the tree, left it, and returned — only to find the chair still there, still in his way. There'd be no fourth time; Ike had made a decision. He sauntered across the patio, past the den window, to the chimney, and there he lifted a leg.

"Ike! Don't — not there!"

His answer? A growl — and while poised on three legs.

In such an instance, a growl directed to one of us is speech. A speech *no*.

But it isn't his protective growl.

When he is defending his people from danger, his growl is full-fledged. And vicious — because he is vicious. A dog has a funda-mental, natural instinct to be protective; it's why man and dog got together in the first place. But many persons are surprised that a Poodle with all his pampered living can be a watchdog. And in-deed he can be.

Dave was shown firsthand about Ike. It was late one night. Brian, Ike, and I had retired. It was before Ike's third Christmas, before we installed Ike's door, before he was penned up again at night. Ike was in his bed, evidently in the midst of a very sound sleep. It must have startled him when Dave came in through the den door. Ike didn't analyze the situation.

Pure instinct, pure fear, pure protectiveness toward home and family lifted him from his bed and streaked him to the middle of the den. He was a snarling, snapping, yelping dog ready to confront the intruder.

In the nick of time Dave realized Ike hadn't recognized him yet. "Ike — it's me!"

Ike broke his charge. According to Dave, there followed an exchange of loving. And a few promises, spoken and unspoken... one of which was that Dave would thereafter in such a situation speak to Ike from the door.

Since that incident we have felt Ike is truly a protector, a watchdog. Just as he proved himself with his door-reporting after our return home, he earned our respect for his middle-of-the-night reports. Twice he has barked Dave to the kitchen to inspect a noise that turned out to be a banging gate. More than likely in both cases a sudden gust of wind blew open the unlatched gate. But, on the other hand, someone could have entered the yard and left when Ike barked.

Another time the gate was firmly latched, but Ike led Dave into a thorough investigation of the yard in the gate area.

At 3:15 A.M. once it wasn't the usual watchdog business that prompted Ike to call Dave to the kitchen. It was, Dave quickly figured out, because of the mournful crying of a cat. I don't know why Ike thought it was necessary to call Dave that time. Maybe he thought his people, too, should hear the wails of the creature out there somewhere in the darkness. Maybe day or night he just didn't want a cat so close to the house.

There is one creature he definitely doesn't want coming to the house night or day. A male stranger. And if the male stranger wears a hat, Ike's animosity is increased.

Ike and I always answer the door together. He stands beside me, on his rear feet, his head even with my waist. I slip my hand under his collar as I open the door. It isn't only to the children at Halloween that Ike gives a formidable impression. He gives it, also to six-foot males. More than one salesman has stumbled back a few steps when the opened door revealed a snarling Ike.

I have observed the crumbling of many a sales pitch as it was delivered to an unreceptive Poodle and a woman who *might* relax her hold on that Poodle's collar.

There is a different kind of hostility toward repairmen. Perhaps it's because I admit them to the house and Ike can sense that they have been summoned. But from a distance he watches every move they make. He barks a constant warning, and if they start toward him, his warning is a deep-throated growl. Most of our repairmen are dog lovers. They try in vain to make friends with Ike. Once they leave, Ike spends much time with their lingering scents — even barks at them. If the same man returns later on another service call, Ike remembers him. He remembers the man, but he gets set once again to be the defender.

Ike is always set to defend in the car. Primed, ready, eyes picking up any advance of male criminals . . . such as the ones at the service stations who commit questionable acts. They sneak up to the back of the car with a big hose (to the front of Dave's VW). They're always rubbing the outside of the windows — followed by a Poodle on the inside who duplicates precisely the route of window travel while he snarls, growls, and barks. The driver's window is never opened beyond a couple of inches . . . even then Ike angrily springs to the window when a presumptuous station attendant pushes the charge ticket through the opening.

It's the same when a male pedestrian comes near the car. Barking, Ike leaps to the window.

It's the same when *any* male comes near — whether riding either a bicycle or motorcycle, or on foot.

It has not always been so. It was not like this at the newsman's corner in California. That man reached inside and petted Ike.

But Ike changed. Maturity brought protectiveness with it. Maturity made him a watchdog.

Maturity and instinct. He was not trained or told to guard us. So also was it his own decision to watch over the meat on the outdoor grill. In his own mind this seemed a logical duty. Every time there's outdoor cooking, Ike is the meat guard. The moment Dave takes the uncooked meat to the patio, Ike takes his position at the base of the grill.

He is on guard duty. He listens, to every sound. He watches. Let not man nor beast nor bird nor bug nor butterfly approach. So great is the honor of a meat guard that when he is left alone with a platter of raw meat, Ike will not touch it.

He expects his people to have a like honor when he has a new yard bone. When it is still meaty and red and juicy and greasy he wants no meddling hands—not even beloved hands. It is not the time or place for frivolity. A new bone is something serious. For a time. When there are no clinging bits of meat remaining, no marrow, and probably no flavor, it is then more like a yard toy than a bone. Now he welcomes people intervention because it isn't much fun to *play* with a yard bone by himself.

Ike is extremely possessive not only of a new yard bone, but of a new house bone, a new rag, a new sock, even a new toy—but only when they are new. The new possession is taken to his bed immediately after presentation, and there it is protected by Ike while he extracts the newness by chewing, or smelling, or caressing, or licking. After he decides the newness is gone, normal treatment is proper.

We're accustomed to this. When we give him a new toy we know it will be a while before we can show him how to play with it. We don't rush him. We are patient.

But Ike is far from patient when he's about to get that new bone, rag, or toy. He's impatient at gift time, whether he is the recipient or not. A package is exciting, as provocative in shipping wrap as in gift wrap. It's still a package regardless of its cover. A package to be opened. A package with something hidden inside. Ike wants the mystery unveiled; Ike wants the package opened. He barks. He looks at the package, at his people. If he can reach it, he paws at the package as he barks. If he can't reach it even standing upright, he paws at the air. If the package remains unopened, intact, still girded in its wrap, it mocks a Poodle with limited patience.

Poodle impatience. The package should be opened. Now.

Urgency. That's the explanation. Impatience comes with urgency.

Urgency...that's when Ike is in the house and hears a come-quickly-to-the-yard-and-investigate sound. Or sees something that simply cannot under any circumstances be ignored.

Come to the yard quickly. So many sounds and sights tell Ike this. A leaf blows by the window. One of his people is in the yard. A dog trots across the front lawn and moves toward the backyard. An audacious cat makes a walkway of the fence. A person is working on a neighbor's roof. All of these are urgent calls. Ike must get outdoors. Now. Right this minute. Impatience in all its power.

Patience, the opposite, is for ordinary requests to get out. Requests to hurry—except on rare occasions when the Poodle warning system was lax. Even if his people are slow to respond, patience is there. Long-suffering Ike. Requests to go out to sun or just sniff around. Requests to go out to wait for the garbage truck (unless he has already heard its roar in the distance—in which case this request moves into the urgent category).

But once the yard has lost its appeal or is no longer needed, Ike knocks at the door.

When he wants in, there is a blend of impatience and patience. Knocking is impatience, but once the door is opened he is patient for the condition check. Maybe in his coat there are long stringy pieces of leaf from the tussocks of pampas grass, tree leaves, or bits of flower stems. These have to be pulled off. And, of course, impossible to overlook are the times when he has rolled in dry grass.

Coat condition may be evident when the door is first opened. However, condition of feet is not so apparent: therefore an inspection must often be made. If there is only a three-inch patch of mud in the entire yard the feet of Ikus P.Q.R.S. Aroonus will be drawn to it.

Foot inspection... Ike is in no hurry. He is submissive. And tolerant. And cooperative. A paw at a time. Lifted in advance by Ike, each paw to be looked at, dusted off with a hand, scrubbed with a dry towel, or a complete foot bath — whatever the condition requires.

Ike knows the condition of his feet before he knocks. When his feet are muddy he never walks by us and enters the house.

"Are your feet dirty, Ike?"

If they are, down goes his head. Down goes Ike. He rolls over. Feet up. Muddy pads visible.

...It was a warm spring day. I didn't think there was any mud in the yard. After Ike went out, as I sometimes do, I left the back door open — just wide enough to admit Ike. When he was ready to come in, he knocked.

"Come on in, Ike," I said. "The door's open."

He didn't come in. I could hear him whine. I discovered why. There were bits of dried mud on a couple of paws.

Good boy.

A good boy deserves a reward. A goody. Well, not *a* goody, but rather two or three before the rewarding is complete. Only *one* goody is almost as bad as not being rewarded at all. *One* goody brings barks, stares at the goody jar, stares at the one who can't count, and a nose shove of the frustration jar.

Good boy. When I wet mop the kitchen floor, Ike is a good boy. He knows. The kitchen is off limits for a time. Later he may bark as he stands at the kitchen door, asking me if the floor is dry yet. But he will not go through that invisible gate. The gate of honor.

There are times when honor is the best disciplinarian for Ikus P.Q.R.S. Aroonus.

One time when we all returned home, Ike, barking steadily, met us at the door. Had he finally jumped over Ike's door? We didn't have long to wonder, because Ike barked us to Ike's door. He showed us. One of the little wire catches had snapped — probably when he had leaned against it. When the catch broke, the door opened wide enough for Ike to pass through. Not a thing in the house had been touched by the accidentally freed Ike. He had been on his honor.

Another time I put Ike's door in place and fastened it, but I forgot to close the door between the kitchen and the foyer. Once again Ike was at the door to greet us when we returned. Barking, he led us all the way through the house to show us he had been a good boy. His honor again...and his joy when able to give us a good report.

There have been times when Ike used his bodily functions as weapons of revenge. There have been also the times of accidents —and the remorse following because he wasn't a *good boy*. One early morning when I opened the kitchen door, I discovered a cowed Ike and also the reason. There were two deposits on the floor. On the floor—not on the round rug under the breakfast table. Never on this rug, for it is special. Ike helped me braid it the last summer we lived in California. Yes, he helped—by lying on the yarn, or the already braided portion, and sometimes by carrying some of the yarn across the room. When he carried it off he was helping: he was either checking it to be certain it was strong enough to be a part of *our* rug, or he was providing his Mommer with an excuse to take a break from such confining work and relax while rewinding yarn. He has never damaged *our* rug. The pad under it, yes, but not the rug.

I was thankful this accident hadn't involved the rug.

"You should have called us, Ike. Shame! Shame! Shame!"

He was in his bed giving in to his despair. He looked as if he had been kicked by a giant foot.

The next morning he met me with glee—extreme glee, even for Ike. He bounced and twirled and led me to the place where the accident of the previous morning had been. Yes, he had been a good boy this morning. No remorse today.

No cringing and slinking away to his bed as yesterday.

He is remorseful, too, those rare times when he has an upset stomach and vomits. It is always as if the very act of regurgitation is a violation of his personal honor. Something over which he has no control shames him greatly. He shows us the spot, then hovers close by while it is cleaned up. He always wears a worried look, one that is not lessened when we assure him—"It's okay."

Remorse cannot exist until there is a wrong, even an unwillful one, followed by guilt. The wrong can be triggered by forgetfulness.

And Ike forgets...possibly because of exuberance.

At times when I have sewing paraphernalia on the guest bed, Ike forgets to ask permission to jump up. Outside a dog barks, or he hears children, or the street sweeper, or a motorcycle, and he jumps up without permission. Or Dave comes home, and Ike brings him to the room — then forgets.

Up. Without asking. Right in the middle of my sewing. The instant his feet touch, he knows. Guilt...full-blown. In the exact same moment, there is remorse.

He jumps down. Immediately. A glance to see if luck is with him, or if I have seen. Tail between his legs. Head so low his shoulder bones push up.

He's sorry. It's never deliberate.

Neither was a wrong deliberate the time Ike and I were playing ball.

For all his dainty Poodle looks, Ike is a masculine dog. When he plays with Dave and Brian he has no reservations. He is all male. He is strong, and tough, and it reflects in his game. Dave and Brian often emerge from the Ike play with scratches on their hands and arms — maybe even a bruise.

But when Ike plays with me, he is gentle. Once in a while, however, there's an accident.

...That one day during a ball game as I was taking the ball from his mouth. Ike adjusted his hold. When he reclamped, he got a finger. Really got a finger. I yelled.

Ike was concerned, obviously concerned.

He licked the finger; he rubbed against my legs; he tried to lick my face; he looked at me searchingly as if he hoped my expression would show the hurt was entirely gone. He gave me his sympathy.

Sympathy given. Sympathy taken.

He freely gives. He freely takes. When Ike is accidentally hurt by one of us, he wants sympathy in the form of elaborate examination, soothing words repeated again, again, and again. He wants stroking and patting.

If he hurts himself he wants sympathy then, too. When he accidentally runs into a piece of furniture, he comes to me. Like a hurt little boy. He lies down at my feet, a front paw extended and trembling with sympathy anticipation.

Sympathy freely taken when he's ill, or just not feeling his best, or if he has had an inoculation. When his ears are bothering him — when he shakes his head or digs at an ear with a rear paw. "That's a shame, such a shame. Does Ike want some ear medicine?" He lies down on his side and paws at an ear. Yes, he wants medicine.

Ike wants sympathy when he is embarrassed:

...That night he howled in his sleep and awakened us. We

rushed to him. He was still in his bed, lying on his side. He looked up sleepily then ducked his head.

...When he spotted the blown-up photograph of a woman's face on a magazine cover and growled at it. And then he knew it was only a picture.

...When he forgets someone has already brought in the newspaper and has to be shown. "See—here's the paper, Ike."

...When he doesn't spot Brian coming out of the school. He can spot from half a block away a small dog camouflaged by landscaping, but he can't always pick out Brian among the other students until Brian gets very close.

It's almost impossible to withhold sympathy from Ike. He looks so miserable and sad when embarrassment touches him.

Ike wants sympathy after a door is *slammed*. This is not the shut door that he so dislikes. This is the door slammed in anger that Ike reacts to. I have to admit I'm the door slammer of the family, and this manifestation of temper upsets Ike. It is as though he thinks my slammed door is to reprimand him for misdeeds of the past, maybe even possible future ones.

Slam. It's like a whip cracked. Wherever he is, regardless of what he's doing, this sound sends him to his bed in a hurry. There he stays, curled up, a circle with head touching tail, until I come to him.

And I've learned to go to him once I've finished with the temper of the slam. If I don't, he stays and stays. I reassure him. "Everything's okay." I pat him. I give him sympathy. And he's happy again.

When I have slammed a door, Ike *wants* me to come to his bed.

But when he is the recluse, I am to stay away; all of us are to stay away.

If he is the recluse in his own bed it is usually because guests kept him up late the night before. Visitors upset his bedtime routine.

If he is the recluse in the car I think it's because once in a great while he likes to be alone. He may ask to be left in the car when we return home. His request is clear. He lies there on the seat and growls when we say, "Come on. Let's go in." He may stay an hour or more before he barks for someone to come get him.

Now for the time being he's had enough of solitary life. Back to the usual. Back to his people. Back to attention, lots of it.

Attention...something on which Poodles thrive...the attention of being brushed or groomed, being fed, being admired by a Poodle-loving female house guest who in Ike's opinion is the perfect new playmate, or being honored by family. If enough attention is not forthcoming, Ike asks for it. He barks, and we respond. "Do you want food?" *No.* "Water?" *No.* "Out?" *No.* "Something put away?" *No.* "A door shut?" *No.*

Attention? Yes.

So important is attention that to receive it, Ike employs ruses.

When I'm working, either at my desk or in the house, and Ike wants me to play with him, he makes tentative requests, showing me his rag, house bone, or ball. If I don't follow through he calls me to another room with his something-is-wrong bark. I can't ignore that; there might be something wrong. And once I'm there, I might as well play....

He uses a looking-for-his-ball ruse. He calls me into the living room. He sniffs under the bookcases, reaches under them with a front paw. I look. No ball. He checks under chairs, behind doors. I do, too. No ball. When we do find his ball, it isn't lost at all. It is in plain sight in the den. He knew it all along, because he didn't even plan to play ball.

Another success is the inspect-me-at-once ruse. Ike scratches madly. I stop my work to inspect the spot. That starts it. He scratches another spot, and another, and another. It takes some time to make a complete body inspection...quite some time.

Which is what he wanted in the first place.

My time. Spent on him. All my attention.

Once Ike had ear trouble in the middle of the night. All three of us answered his distress barks. He was soothed by the application of ear powder. He quit scratching, quit shaking his head. Until we started to leave. The itching mysteriously returned every time we turned away. Such a pitiful look he had. We wouldn't leave him in such misery, would we? Well, not right away.

We're not sure if it were all ruse, or half ruse and half legitimate, or all legitimate. He *does* have ear trouble. On the other hand, he *does* stoop to Poodle trickery.

I doubt if Ike himself would accept the *trickery* premise. It shouldn't be considered wrong, should it, for a Poodle to make sure he has maximum attention from his people?

Attention. He wants it in great amounts when it's about to be denied him for the length of our pending absence. "You'll stay, Ike. You have to go to bed." He goes to his bed, awaits our attention. Before we leave we pet him; we speak lovingly in soft voices; we cultivate a serene mood. We learned a long time ago that to leave him in a turmoil was to ask for mischief. If one of us stands back, Ike with a clawing foot beckons that person to join the Ike cult.

Great amounts of attention when we return, especially if it is night and bedtime when we come back home. His happiness when he sees us is not like the outlandish daytime exhibition. The initial jubilance is brief—then it's time for loving. From each one of us. And then? Hurry time—okay, that's routine. But not back to bed again. Not so soon. He refuses to settle down for the night until he has had the benefit of our company for at least thirty minutes or so.

Our returning-from-an-evening-out attention was redefined on one occasion. Friends, with whom we had spent the evening, came in for coffee. When they left—an hour or so later—Dave and I put Ike to bed and went to our bedroom.

Ike began to whine.

He had been cheated. When we came home our attention had gone to the guests—not to Ike.

Dave left the bedroom. He returned with Ike in his arms. Poor mistreated, lonely Poodle. We petted him. Several times Ike with a curved paw pulled one of our hands to his chest for scratching. We talked to him. He talked to us. *Uh-huh.*

Now he went peacefully to bed. Though delayed, the welcome-home ritual had been performed.

A need for people-loving. For attention. Full measure. A demand, and a fulfillment.

What about a desire for Poodle-loving? How does it work turned around? "Come here, Ike." And that may be the time he chooses to be aloof in the exasperating way Poodles have. He looks, then turns and walks away. "Here. Come." Spoken to a retreating Poodle rear. It makes a scene like a foreign movie with the wrong sound dubbed in.

"Come!" Sternly and insistently. Eventually he comes.

But the next time he may react with aloofness again—unless loving from us is something he himself wants at that particular moment.

The way he reacts—in this or any other situation—is always individual.

His own way. The way of Ikus P.Q.R.S. Aroonus.

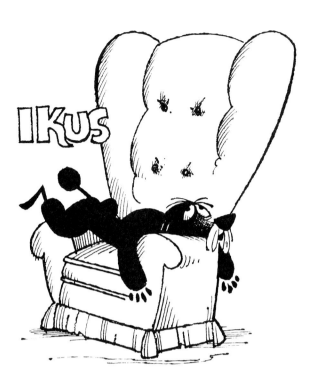

CHAPTER FOURTEEN

IT HAPPENS OFTEN, almost nightly — a little family vignette.

...Ike is in the wing chair, his head propped on the arm. He begins. His eyes rest on the first face, the one closest to him. People words come. "Pretty boy. Ikus is such a fine boy."

Ike answers. With a sound. Basso, somewhere between a purr and a moan.

Then his eyes move slowly to the second face, pause there, waiting... *asking* for more people words. "Pretty boy...." Words acknowledged.

To the third face then, the last one. That completes Ike's inventory. His loving inventory.

Of his family. The family of Ikus P.Q.R.S. Aroonus.

Ike's loving inventory is like saying to each of us: *I give my love to you.* He gives. And we accept it.

We don't take an inventory as Ike does. But we know he's there.

I especially know he's there...the many hours he spends at my side when we're alone. The constancy of Ikus is a gift from him to me. And I accept it with gratitude.

He's there. When I'm afraid. He knows. And he may be afraid, too.

...It was storming. Ike and I stood at the window. I looked out at the signs of turbulence and was alarmed. Ike pushed between the window and me. He was trembling. He was scared, but he barked at the weather then looked at me. It was as if he said, *Don't worry, Mommer. I'll protect you.*

He's there. When I'm ill. He stays on the bed with me — except When Dave and Brian are eating. But even during a meal he comes to the bedroom door once or twice to see if I'm all right.

He's there. When I work at the desk. Weekday, holiday, night, Sunday — he's always there if I am.

He's there. When I'm in the kitchen. Or any room. Even in a closet if it's necessary that I be in a closet.

He's there. When I'm in the bathroom. Or, as is often the case, he may anticipate my routine and precede me there.

He's there. When I make the bed. Either he's on the bed, to be moved off. Or by the bed, underfoot...stretched out full length in the pathway around the bed. He dozes. He knows I'll step around him. He knows I would never deliberately step on him. He knows because he trusts me.

He trusts his family.

His trust is like a small expensive gift laid in an open palm.

The gift of trust from Ikus. We accept it.

Ikus...our loving name for Ike...a name for a member of the family.

And we are a family. It's as simple as that. A family of four. The three of us and Ikus...little boy Poodle.

Like a little boy he may fall asleep with his toys. He likes to lie down on his rag or his sock, or with his head against his ball or one of his house bones.

Once we watched him pick up his rag by a corner and, dragging it like a toddler's dirty blanket, he crossed the room, plopped down on the rag and went to sleep.

Little boy Poodle.

Little lost boy Poodle....

I went from the kitchen to the guest room. Ike came after me, but I was already out of sight. He went to the master bedroom where he thought I had gone. I saw him return to the hall, heard his tags jingle as he walked back to the kitchen. Then back down the hall. He passed the guest room door but still didn't see me. I could have spoken to him, but I didn't.

I wanted to watch.

Back into the master bedroom he went. When he returned again to the hall he was beginning to trot. He missed seeing me again — his head was held straight, his eyes followed the exact route he had taken before.

Once again to the kitchen, then back.

The trot quickened. It was the first settling in of panic.

He was lost. Little lost boy Poodle couldn't find his Mommer.

He was hunting me as a child would. He was not tracking me by scent.

I spoke. "Here, Ikus." He ran to me. He jumped. He licked my face and hands. He barked. He danced. He groaned.

He had found me. He wasn't lost any longer. Where there had been sadness there was now joy.

How utterly dependent is this Poodle. His dependency we accept. We accepted it that day a long time ago when instead of three we became four.

For, in spite of his bravado, Ikus P.Q.R.S. Aroonus needs so much from people.

I hope for his sake someone is always there. . . .